NO REGRETS

REFLECTIONS OF A PRESIDENTIAL SPOKESMAN

D1413220

WIMAR WITOELAR

NO REGRETS

REFLECTIONS OF A PRESIDENTIAL SPOKESMAN

EQUINOX
PUBLISHING
JAKARTA SINGAPORE

Equinox Publishing (Asia) Pte. Ltd.
PO Box 6179 JKSGN
Jakarta 12062, Indonesia

www.EquinoxPublishing.com

ISBN 979-95898-4-3

First Equinox Edition 2002

1 3 5 7 9 10 8 6 4 2

for Gus Dur

THE END
AND
THE BEGINNING

The End Comes and I'm Not There

This, I thought, is living as it is supposed to be. Soaking in a bathtub in a luxury suite bathroom designed for the opulent, looking out the window at the world above and below. No matter that I did not pay for the room, I still felt very rich. No other sensation can match a high-rise view of Darling Harbour and Sydney Bridge, postcard pretty in one of the most charming cities in the world. This was surrealistically distant from the reality from which I was extracted to meet a one-year commitment to speak in Sydney. Reality for me was Indonesia, a nation torn by strife, trying to pull away from the oppression of three decades by the darkly masterful Soeharto regime.

Reality was a politically frail yet mentally fit president trying to remain in control in Jakarta. However, this fitness did not help against the cabal forged by special interests. It was match point in a game without an umpire.

President Abdurrahman Wahid was about to be ousted, and I was caught away from him. I was the Chief Presidential Spokesman, and we thought we still had a week before the special session of the People's Consultative Assembly, Indonesia's 'super parliament', would convene to issue their final verdict on the long-standing impasse between the president and Parliament. But the new attorney general, straight-shooter Marsillam Simandjuntak, was preparing for a wide-scale investigation of allegedly corrupt officials. This was Saturday, 21 July 2001 and I knew some of the investigations would start the following Monday. But events superceded these plans when Assembly Chairman Amien Rais pre-empted the process and announced a series of steps which would limit President Wahid's options in keeping his constitutional responsibilities.

The only recourse for President Wahid was to call on the people and ask the Assembly to account for their adherence to the constitution. That would mean a presidential decree freezing Parliament and preparing for a special election. Knowing the interests of the military and the police and the ambition of the politicians in Parliament, I knew the decree would not be supported. The Wahid presidency was coming to an end, and I was six thousand miles away—helplessly soaked in material comfort in this bathtub in the sky.

I Wasn't There in the Beginning, Either

Not quite two years earlier in October 1999, I found myself in New York City. The law firm of Baker-McKenzie in collaboration with the Asia Society had invited me to speak at several forums for American-Indonesian societies in New York, Houston and Los Angeles.

I left Jakarta with every prediction indicating that soon Megawati Soekarnoputri would be the president of Indonesia. I liked the idea because it would present a clean break from the Soeharto regime. We also saw that Gus Dur had given his support to Megawati, which was a logical consequence of the fact that they had been political partners for a long time, practically since the early nineties when Megawati became a political figure. Their friendship strengthened when Megawati began to face persecution by the Soeharto regime. Gus Dur himself did not show any presidential ambitions, although we knew he was a man who would never resist the call of his country, especially when urged to play a role by his closest constituencies.

I had nothing to do with the presidential election. I was not a member of the Assembly and I was not campaigning for any particular candidate. I felt Habibie would be blocked by the public's resentment against the Soeharto regime, and anyone outside that regime should be given a shot at the presidency as long as their political support was based on a repudiation of the corrupt and violent past. So when the US tour came up I felt I could leave the country, choosing instead with anticipation the challenges of bringing Indonesian perspectives to the public in the United States.

One day before I left on 19 October 1999 something came up which almost made me change my plans. Susanto Pudjomartono, chief editor of the *Jakarta Post*, called me to say that Megawati had agreed to appear as a guest on a television talk show. This would be a rare occurrence indeed; Megawati having been ever so silent since the beginning of her political career and especially in the days leading to her possible ascendancy to the highest position in the land. There was a catch, though. Susanto reported Megawati as saying that she was only willing to appear on the condition that I was chosen to be the moderator. I don't know if this was Susanto or Megawati talking but in any case I was flattered. For a talk show host this would be a big scoop professionally. It is a privilege to be mentioned by name by someone of such high standing in national politics. But the flight schedule did not allow me to do both the TV show and keep my speaking engagement in New York, where the audience already had been invited for the Asia Society event. So I had to present my apologies to Susanto and suggested a competent substitute to take my place, my friend Bambang Harymurti, chief editor of *Tempo*.

So there I was at the Asia House in upper Manhattan. They put me in as the luncheon speaker, sort of an entertainer-cum-commentator role, after a morning of serious presentations. I made remarks which were very much reflective of my feelings of elation at the prospect of leaving the Soeharto-Habibie regime. In the Q&A we speculated on what a Megawati government would be like.

The next day I made another speaking appearance, this time in Houston, Texas. In between the event sessions, I called my office in Jakarta and spoke with Lila, my press manager. She blurted out, "Wimar! Our president is Gus Dur!" I never did find out whether the exclamatory tone was due to joy or despair, but everybody was caught by surprise when Gus Dur was elected instead of Megawati, his political sister. I was very surprised myself, but not disappointed because they were both on the same side of the division between the Soeharto system and the new Indonesia.

Gus Dur and Megawati both had constituencies committed to reform, but most importantly, they gave the people the hope of a new leadership. We knew that the job of reform would always be a task for civil society as a whole, rather than for any individual leader. In Houston my talk revolved around the idea of Gus Dur and how his presidency would differ from Megawati's. There were speculation as to who would be the vice president, to be elected the day after the president was elected. Again I missed on that projection. Although the name Megawati was considered, I thought that she would play a different role and that Gus Dur would have to use the vice presidency to accommodate other political streams. Demonstrations, some of them rather violent, showed us that Megawati's followers in the Indonesian Democratic Party of Struggle (PDI-P) and the masses were deeply disappointed when Megawati wasn't elected president. Street riots especially in places like Jakarta and Bali soon made it apparent that Gus Dur had no choice but to accept Megawati's election as vice president, which is a choice he did not mind at all. So soon enough they were inaugurated with fanfare and full support from the Parliament, from the Assembly, from the press, from the public and from the international community.

∽∾

In all of my years away from Indonesia, this was absolutely my proudest moment to be Indonesian. At the time I happened to be writing a column for *Newsweek* at their request. Presenting that column here is probably the best way to sum up my feelings at the beginning of the Wahid presidency:

LISTEN TO OUR HOPEFUL HEARTS

It's no joke: Indonesians are proud of our silent princess and
her mercurial mentor

By Wimar Witoelar

When Gus Dur predicted more than a year ago that he would
become the next president of Indonesia, it seemed like some
kind of political joke. Nobody ever doubted Gus Dur's
intelligence. But Megawati Soekarnoputri seemed assured of
riding a popular wave to the top position. She remained remote
and aloof, while others toiled in unpopular back-room politics.
To our amazement, the joke came true, and Megawati's
coronation didn't happen. It turned out that mastery of the
institutional political process counts, for better or for worse.
President Gus Dur, as Wahid is known, and Vice President
"Sister Mega" are now again a political couple—quite a
romantic ending to our Indonesian fairy tale.

To the outsider, they are a most unlikely pair to lead
our nation of 200 million out of its troubles. We face the worst
economic collapse in modern times, widely publicized atrocities
by the military in East Timor and less-known violence against
our own people. Yet upon their election, my eldest brother sent
a joyous e-mail to me in capital letters: "I HAVE REGAINED
MY PRIDE TO BE INDONESIAN."

Who can help being proud? As a people, we have gone
against a harsh regime and elected the first-ever pair of Indonesian
leaders without the customary props of military power,
bureaucratic support and financial clout. So who cares if the
outsiders call our new president a "frail cleric"? Let them call the
separately elected vice president a princess who is silent like the
Sphinx. They suspect she is incompetent, though she led a party
in silent resistance to mighty President Soeharto and led her party
to victory with more votes than there are people in two Australias.

For us, it is the people who won. Never mind that the Assembly, which delivered the final vote, was full of political betrayals and horse trading. Had we gone back a number of years, this odd couple would be our undisputed icons of integrity. Now all they have to do is shake off the labels of Machiavellianism (for Gus Dur) and vanity (for Megawati). The proof, as they say, is in the pudding, and the pudding is not the presidency but the regaining of confidence as a nation. We, the people, may be allowed to gloat a little. We may enjoy this irrational moment, because our world had gone crazy: currencies falling, banks failing, heads being chopped off and neighbors demonizing millions for the crimes of a few. "Barbarians," said a foreign reporter, citing his countrymen's image of Indonesians. Well, no more.

But the foreign investor asks, how do you actually get out of the hole? Obviously, by managing an economic recovery and political rejuvenation. Are Gus Dur and Mega competent? Who knows? They have never been tested. They are not rocket scientists. They will preside; mere mortals will manage. Once these mortals are appointed, we will judge whether Indonesia is safe for the foreign investor and for their families to shop in the malls of Jakarta.

Gus Dur and Mega may have shortcomings in competence, even in character, but the able men and women who didn't vote for our rocket-scientist former presidents will give a helping hand. The princess and her mentor will attract bright young economists and managers, not people of dubious character who lingered around BJ Habibie, our Ph.D. ex-president.

Gus Dur is weak in physique, mercurial in temperament. Maybe that is why he dared to maneuver against the powerful political establishments, stood firm against Islamic zealots from his own world and was not shy to face down students. He negotiated, cajoled, danced like Rudolf Nureyev and became president without firing a single shot. Had she been smart enough to translate her millions of popular support into a vote-getting coalition on the Assembly floor, Mega would have been president. She is perceived to be stony and remote. But she does have infinite patience, and impeccable motherliness; she is an upper-middle-class woman who relates to the downtrodden. She is either a princess or a queen mother, but she could not get the electoral votes to become a queen. Well, maybe alongside Gus Dur she is a queen. They have been an item for many years. Mega's husband says Gus Dur is her mentor.

What is wonderful is that with unbelievable alacrity, our drama has all been resolved in such reconciliatory tones. Mega thanking Habibie; Hamzah Haz, Mega's rival, praising Mega; even Habibie bowing out gracefully and Wiranto keeping out of trouble. Now we need both truth and reconciliation. We have reconciliation. Let us eventually get the truth—or at least some of it. This is a honeymoon. May it last for a finite period, because then we will move on and start electing leaders whom the world, in its conventional taste, can understand without listening to our hearts.

Why don't we elect the best and the brightest? The Ph.D.s, the educated, the supermanagers, the professionals? Because we need heart, and stamina and a sense of destiny. Being president of Indonesia is not a well-defined job; it comes with no retirement plan. It is as life-threatening as any modern disease. It is not amazing that Indonesia has such difficulty finding leaders. What is more amazing is that anyone would expect conventional leaders to emerge from a 33-year system designed to reduce people to uniform mediocrity. Look what happened to outstanding people during Soeharto's reign. Look what robotic monsters he created to support—and to continue briefly—his demonic system.

For better or for worse, the princess and her mentor
are joined by the desperate hope of their people.

Newsweek, 1 November 1999

Caught by Surprise

I was in Sydney that fateful July day to honor a
commitment made a year before to the New South Wales
Centenary of Federation Committee. They were organizing a multitude of events in commemoration of
Australia's 100th anniversary as a federation. One feature
of the celebration was a series of five public lectures by
speakers from five continents. As I was the only
representative from Asia, the honor was significant. Still
I was in doubt in that week in July 2001 whether to go
ahead with my plans or stand by in Jakarta for President
Wahid's crucial days. My speech was scheduled for 25 July
2001. The special session of the Assembly was scheduled
for 1 August and I figured that I could fulfill my duties
on 25 July and still make it back to Jakarta in time. Besides,
Australia was an important place for us politically. The
Indonesian government was engaged in a serious effort to
rebuild bilateral relations with Australia. We had friends
who could support our cause in the media and the
academic community in Sydney.

I asked Gus Dur whether I should stay or I should
go. He never hesitated, he thought I should go. At the last
minute before leaving the president's office for the airport,
I paused in the doorway for a few seconds and asked, "Gus,
are you *sure* I should leave for Australia?" He answered,
"Yes, go. It is very important that you keep your
commitment. Things are going to be fine here, don't
worry." But only five steps away from his office, one of

the presidential aides ran after me and said the president asked me to come back, he had something to say. I went back not knowing what to expect, but a smile must have crept across my taut face as the president asked me, "Wimar, if you have the chance could you look for some audio books for me? Anything as long as it is not John Steinbeck's *Of Mice and Men*, because I just finished that. But make your choice, you know what I like."

∽∾

Most of us around the presidential office were surprised when the Assembly accelerated their special session. We had miscalculated and totally underestimated the desperation of the political elite who had everything to gain by getting rid of their political thorn in the side. No matter that Gus Dur was a legally elected, legitimate president—the first one the nation had ever had. Many officials with vested interests had everything to lose had they allowed the law to be upheld. Several top officials of the Soeharto regime were being investigated by the Wahid government. Ginandjar Kartasasmita, the allegedly corrupt anchor of several of Soeharto's cabinets over the last twenty years, had recently been indicted. Soeharto's son Tommy had been convicted and then went into hiding, a fugitive of the law. The screws of justice were tightening around many who ironically are officials of current legislature and political parties. It is no coincidence that these problematic figures were also leading the movement to get Gus Dur out of official power.

Weeks after Parliament turned us out of office I said half-jokingly to Marsillam Simandjuntak (who had spent exactly one working day as the attorney general) that he was probably the reason the Assembly moved up their special session from 1 August to 23 July. Unlike many of his predecessors, Marsillam was regarded as serious about enacting legal prosecution against big corruption cases involving government officials in the Soeharto regime. But in that sad week in July these hopes were again betrayed. Instead of the government cracking down on corruption, we saw Parliament taking the reformist government out of action.

Indonesia's political crisis peaked the night of Sunday 22 July into the early morning hours of Monday 23 July. President Wahid issued a decree to dissolve Parliament, and to hold fresh parliamentary elections within one year as well as dissolve Golkar, the political party which had been Soeharto's key piece of political infrastructure. As I was away in Sydney, my colleague Yahya B. Staquf, assistant spokesman, read the decree in a firm voice over the nation's television and radio airwaves. It seemed to be just what the other side was waiting for. Barely concealing his excitement, Assembly Chairman Amien Rais responded in an instant and told the Assembly members, the military and the police to ignore the decree. In defiance of their constitutional role the military and the police withheld their support from their supreme commander, the nation's president. The president, powerless to stop the renegade lawmakers, waited calmly in the Presidential Palace.

Later in the day when Gus Dur was no longer president according to the Assembly, thousands of people came streaming into the palace. It was, by eyewitness accounts, a touching scene. Many who had been with-holding support for the beleaguered president came, some in tears, to express their sympathy. A touch of surrealism was added as Megawati's security guards started to come in and take control. Presidential staff who usually went about their business roaming freely in the palace compound had to get used to the cold stares and less friendly commands of the new security force. Outside in the political world, nobody lifted a finger as Indonesia's *reformasi* went off the tracks. Mark Bowling, the Australian Broadcasting Commission's correspondent in Jakarta reported on television, "The impeachment juggernaut is being driven by his former enemies and his former allies." Then in response to a question from the ABC news anchor, Bowling said President Wahid was "actually not accused of any wrongdoing."

A military show of strength accompanied that day's crucial session of Parliament. Forty thousand soldiers and police were deployed amid fears that the latest political crisis would erupt into bloodshed. In a shameful choice now regretted by many of their own, the military and police had clearly taken sides in the political standoff. Instead of standing by and remaining politically neutral, the military in one case literally aimed their cannons at the Presidential Palace while troops at the Parliament Building positioned themselves to protect the sessions going on inside. President Wahid was politically isolated. Key generals publicly opposed the presidential decree. Police in Jakarta had been directly ordered by the head of the National Police to disobey the decree. The seven hundred members of the People's Consultative Assembly were geared to hold the impeachment on that Monday. They gathered to demand that President Wahid account for his turbulent twenty-one months in office. But the president had already stated he would not respond to such a request, as there was no constitutional or legal reason to demand such an accountability report. The Assembly decided if that was the case then Vice President Megawati Soekarnoputri would be installed to replace him as president. And indeed she was: the daughter of Soekarno, who was ousted by forces behind General Soeharto, now became president with the enthusiastic support of many of the holdovers from the Soeharto regime.

∽∽

Away from the political noise, Jakarta was physically quiet. Early in the morning of 23 July dozens of tanks thundered down the main boulevard connecting the Hotel Indonesia roundabout to the large square surrounding Monas (Monumen Nasional), the Soekarno-designed main monument in the city center facing the Presidential Palace. The tanks veered off in different directions and police-military units stood guard at most of the main roads of the city. A very heavy military presence surrounded the Parliament Building and senior generals declared their main purpose was to protect the Parliament and the People's Consultative Assembly and make sure the parliamentarians could work peacefully.

As ABC's Bowling said on television, ironically the charges against President Wahid were extremely nebulous and unsubstantiated. Accused by politicians and parts of the press of corrupt activities involving several cases, Gus Dur was never proven of any wrongdoing by any court of law. An investigative committee within Parliament— whose political bias is obvious—had raised the allegations. In fact the parliamentary leaders perverted their mandate with just one thing in mind: the removal of President

Wahid. Tellingly, Amien Rais, when asked by another Australian television journalist if the impeachment process against President Wahid was legitimate, replied, "The People's Consultative Assembly is the supreme body of the nation. Whatever it does is legitimate."

The bottom line is that at last a handful of politicians, elements of the military and some parliamentary leaders succeeded in their year-long campaign to oust President Wahid from power. The tanks across town and the parliamentarians wielding extra-parliamentary power operated much in the style of the transfer of power from Soekarno to Soeharto. It was déjà vu. Soeharto's regime all over again, only this time it came to power not just with soldiers on the streets, but also with the full cooperation of the politicians in Parliament.

∽∾

The end of Gus Dur's presidency was as sudden as the beginning. Less than two years after my proudest moment, here I was sitting in a hotel room in Sydney—silently watching the internet news, email and cell phone SMS messages during the midnight hours of 21 July 2001. The political elite betrayed the 'hopeful hearts' of my column and replaced Gus Dur with Megawati Soekarnoputri, now reprogrammed by a pragmatic political alliance. It is a story of a nation's detour to democracy, and for me it is also an intensely personal one.

My story is one of a fascinating experience which would not have been possible without the kindness and trust of many, only a few of whom I can mention here. First of all this book must be dedicated to the greatest man I have ever known, Abdurrahman Wahid—whose trust is so implicit that I have not consulted him once in the writing of this book. Then the list of good people is endless. The role of presidential spokesman would not have been mine if I were not convinced of its usefulness by the encouragement of Yenny Wahid and Greg Barton and the trust of Marsillam Simandjuntak. So many people were extremely kind and supportive during my months of service with the president: the Wahid family including brother Dr. Umar Wahid and his team of presidential doctors, General Amir Tohar, Colonel Muhadi, Major Chandra and all the professional security personnel assigned to the president. All cabinet members provided instant access and it was a pleasure to work with most of them. The media never gave up their friendship with me and I gained many friends in the international press, especially in Australia. Closest to me were my fellow spokesmen Yahya B. Staquf and Adhie Massardi, persons I had never known before who turned out to be the best I could hope to work with. Trusted assistant Santo Dewatmoko, a geologist and management graduate whom I privately recruited, kept me away from discouraging bureaucratic details. All respect and gratitude go to Hani Hasyim, the producer who became manager of my public persona. She with Dwiyana Handayani and staff kept our communications company going as I disappeared from the private sector for ten months.

But through it all, my world revolves around my family. To my wife Suvatchara who left her homeland for this messy (but hopeful) country, and to my wonderful sons Satya and Aree, I publicly declare my total indebtedness to them for never flinching from unqualified support and allowing me to lead an interesting life. In a wider perspective, my brothers Luki, Toerki and Rachmat and my dear sister Kiki have maintained the family closeness our parents created, which is an important stabilizing factor.

A special note of thanks go to Greg Barton again and Mark Hanusz of Equinox Publishing who gave me the idea to write this book, providing me total freedom while unhesitatingly jumping in to clean up parts which had become messy because of my enthusiasm. Last but not least, credit goes to Sari P. Setiogi for her assistance in the preparation of this manuscript and Clara Lila Damayanthi for her loyal rescue work in the final moments. The responsibility for the remaining short-comings is entirely mine.

PART ONE

THE SETTING

A Slice of History

By the year 2000, the Byzantine politics of Indonesia were tangled to the extreme and history itself caught us as bewildered as innocent deer in fast-moving traffic. Despite the glamour of President Soekarno's 'non-aligned' and fiercely independent leadership, Indonesia had become one of the poorest countries in the world by the mid-1960s. We had to line up for anything from gasoline to sugar while black markets were the standard way for obtaining US Dollars, train tickets and television sets. Our per capita income had sunk below that of many African and Asian countries. There had been little economic growth as politics dominated the first twenty-five years since independence in 1945. We had become acquainted with shortages and hyperinflation, and Indonesia had begun to disengage from the world community. Soekarno took Indonesia out of the United

Nations and the Olympic Games and set up the CONEFO (Conference of the New Emerging Forces) and GANEFO (Games of the New Emerging Forces), bold concepts going against the global mainstream. Today you can find people in their late thirties with names like 'Ganefiati' inspired by the 1963 GANEFO, an Olympic-like event in Jakarta where Indonesia came in third place. Likewise, many babies were named after heroes of that period such as Patrice Lumumba and Fidel Castro, just as there are older people named Hitler and Mussolini. Everybody was poor. As a teenager I was molded by the psychology of deprivation—cursed with an irrational desire to cherish plastic bags and complimentary ballpoints pens, even until this very day.

No one at that time imagined that just thirty years later Indonesia would be an Asian tiger, one of the Newly Industrialized Countries, an Asian Miracle Economy with fast cars, fast roads and fast money. The sixfold expansion of the Indonesian economy during the Soeharto period, and projections that it could become the world's fifth-largest economy by the year 2020, were unthinkable when we were crowding in trains that took us a day and a half to get from Solo to Jakarta—barely five hundred kilometers away. The three decades of the Soeharto government (dubbed the 'New Order' as we referred to Soekarno's time as the 'Old Order') were blessed by one of the highest economic growth rates in the world. That was the good news. The bad news was that most Indonesian people did not share the pleasures of this economic miracle and have remained rock-bottom poor. This bred a culture of acceptance. And it created a new feudal class based around the bureaucracy, the military and, most of all, money.

It was not surprising that this artificial economy also concealed structural faults such as a dangerous imbalance between production and consumption, poor development of human resources, excessive leverage and financial pyramiding and a general lack of sustainability. Towards the end of 1997, as Indonesia's economic Titanic steamed on seemingly impervious to danger, everything collapsed without warning. The fall of the economic house of cards was precipitated by the Asian financial crisis, but the roots of the collapse lie deep in Indonesian society. The drastic reversal was staggering. The single-year collapse in growth is among the largest ever recorded anywhere in the world. Millions of Indonesians lost the jobs they had from the 'trickle-down' economy of the New Order. Investors fled and are still shying away from the country which had been an investment paradise for thirty years. Almost overnight, the banking system collapsed and thousands of firms went bankrupt. The stock market became a sample library of the vagaries of financial markets. Economically, Indonesia became the Land of the Living Dead.

∽∾

Indonesia's economic façade was disguised for thirty-two years by the political camouflage of New Order democracy with the political group Golkar as the kingpin of the system. Virtually the operating system of the Soeharto hardware, Golkar's pseudo-democracy had more bugs than any version of Microsoft Windows. Clients had no recourse each time the system crashed, only to be invariably rebooted by financial sleight of hand, coercion and application of raw power. Human rights violations abounded, far more than just the East Timor violations to which the Western powers were so sensitive. As the world wakes up to international terror, many forget that the purely domestic brand of arrests, press closures, and killings done by our government have caused systematic damage on a scale beyond the wildest imaginings of the most cunning of terrorists. The gentle quality of the Indonesian population belied the harsh and ruthless character of the regime that ruled its life. When the economic crisis hit in 1997, the human rights violators were caught unprepared. The world got a glimpse of the obscene underlayer of Soeharto power—which was threatened with exposure by the Wahid government— when just in time the Megawati government gave the hard-liners hope of burying their sins.

Reformasi and Soeharto's End

The era of *reformasi*, the catchword by which the reform movement came to be known, surfaced in 1996 but soon after changed character. In 1996 resistance to the New Order regime took up the cause of persistence against repression. On 27 July 1996 this attitude received a very strong impetus from the government's awkward handling of the PDI affair, which culminated in the storming of the PDI Secretariat on Jalan Diponegoro. That single event transformed PDI Chairwoman Megawati from just a politician coasting on the name of her famous father into an full-fledged opposition leader. Her stock in trade was a stolid, rock hard, nonviolent and resistant style. Actually Megawati had been a parliament member since 1992. In fact, she was nominated by then-chairman of PDI, Suryadi, and like all rookies in the formal political system gained her parliament seat with the approval of President

Soeharto. But when Suryadi assumed a pro-government stance and entered into conflict with Megawati, she was thrust into the role of the people's champion.

This was a sad situation at that time, but it proved to be the source of immense political capital for her political career. Her credentials as opposition leader was qualitatively enhanced with the storming of the PDI Secretariat. Scores of party members loyal to Megawati died in the massacre jointly conducted between Suryadi's PDI followers, undercover Soeharto operators, and not-so-undercover protection by the military. The valiant struggle ended in tragedy but '27 July' became the battle cry of the Megawati movement which carried her all the way to the presidency. Ironically the investigation into the military's involvement, which was impossible in the Soeharto period, was never endorsed by Megawati herself, and when she ascended to the presidency she appeared to forget about the case altogether, not even appearing for the annual commemoration of this tragedy. Some of the alleged perpetrators of the attack are now good friends of Megawati and her husband.

The other stream of opposition came from Amien Rais, leader of the respected Muslim cultural organization Muhammadiyah. Amien had started to adopt a militant and courageous position against President Soeharto even though he gained his chairmanship with Soeharto support in 1993. He started to express an alternative platform for the political future of the nation. Because of his base in Yogyakarta and Muhammadiyah he enjoyed implicit support from his students and academic community, in addition to his Muslim urban Muhammadiyah membership.

The third force which provided the real dynamics of *reformasi* consisted of a loosely organized but highly enthusiastic and sincere student movement. Finding their base on campuses, like the University of Indonesia, Gadjah Mada University and to a lesser extent in other universities, the students started to flex their muscles by going out into the streets and campaigning on pressing political issues with the common aim of challenging the government.

In the meantime the Soeharto regime became more belligerent. Evidence of overconfidence also started to show. With the usual five-year mandate which the Assembly had given him in 1998, Soeharto appointed a cabinet which seemed totally oblivious to the changing mood of the population. It was even more narrowly-based and cynical than any of Soeharto's previous cabinets. He appointed people like Bob Hasan—a household name synonymous with corruption and privilege—to the crucial position of minister of industry and trade. He even appointed his own daughter to the position of minister of social affairs. It was not in itself an important post, but because of the political culture at that time, Tutut transformed the ministry into an institution to which other ministers had to pay allegiance on the pretext of mobilizing funds for social affairs. She was, in effect, the bagwoman of President Soeharto, with a very thin disguise of legality.

The arbitrary policies of the Soeharto regime were never formally criticized in the press, but street talk and the mood in various forums such as seminars, discussions and especially the internet, branded Soeharto as an oppressor and his political death warrant was slowly being drawn up by the civil society networks. The final execution of the regime came about rather fortuitously because of the financial crisis which had crept in from Thailand, spreading to surrounding economies where the level of financial leverage was unsustainably high. The Indonesian economy was operating quite well, but the foundation was corruption and privilege. This made Indonesia exceptionally vulnerable to financial instability and ultimately saw the value of the Indonesian economy plummet in the eyes of the creditor nations and the international business community.

By mid-1997, the situation had become a full-blown crisis and criticism against the regime could be launched quite vocally on the basis of economic issues. The public began to point the finger directly at Soeharto himself as an incompetent and failed head of government. In this setting, students stepped up their demonstrations and Amien Rais stepped up his barnstorming in public rallies. Megawati did what she does best—saying nothing but basking in her martyr image as the most formidable opponent of the New Order because of her party's persecution in the 27 July 1996 attack. When Soeharto finally fell and surrendered the presidency to Habibie, who was part of the Soeharto regime without the extreme powers which Soeharto had, all three movements were in play: the student movement, Amien Rais' political movements and Megawati as the silent beneficiary of anti-Soeharto sentiment.

Gus Dur's own organization, Nahdlatul Ulama, a grassroots Islamic organization with thirty or forty million members, did not take an explicit political position on the issue of *reformasi*. However, because they had consistently lived the values central to *reformasi* such as human rights, pluralism and political freedom, they were also seen to be very much a part of the reform movement. Soeharto fell without an heir and Habibie stumbled into the void, never being able to find the right form even until the end. But in this political vacuum Indonesians won freedom of the press, freedom for political prisoners and started a public discourse to build a new political system.

The massive power structure built around Soeharto by the military and Golkar was quite confused as to what it would do next, while the Megawati loyalists basically stood still preparing for the elections. Amien Rais was agile in his political maneuvering but his problem was his closeness to Habibie and ICMI (The Association of Muslim Intellectuals), which the new regime used for legitimization. It was this closeness that damaged Amien's claim to be a true reformer, as he could not show himself to be independent. His opposition to the Soeharto regime faded when Soeharto's hand-picked successor took over.

The main hope of the reform movement was to build a civil society which was beginning to grow on the strength of various NGOs with liberal democratic ideas such as good governance, human rights, the environment, and gender issues. Support organizations grew with moral and financial support from NGOs in the liberal democracies. When Gus Dur came to power the map changed for these organizations. Amien Rais' supporters went outside the power center, after trying for one year to keep their toehold in the coalition cabinet. Megawati's party showed an amazing lack of competence, both in the parliamentary processes (which caused her to lose the presidency) and in defining her role in government. Never expressing her real desires and concealing the intense frustration inside her own party, she became a smoldering, silent partner. The Gus Dur-Megawati match may have been made in heaven, but the winds of hell were blowing just beneath the surface.

The students and the civil society basically shared Gus Dur's ideals, but being outside the government their standards were normative and naïvely unrealistic. Without active support from his natural constituency, Gus Dur's government was forced to search for support among people jockeying for position. Many people came asking for assignments but they were not necessarily good people. Many good people were recruited but often were ineffective in the government although loyal and well-intentioned.

∾

The last three years have seen two instances of regime change. In late 1998, Soeharto stepped aside against a backdrop of the previous May's riots—widespread violence provoked by professional agents. It started with bloody police-military action against students and continued with arson and looting in Jakarta and communal clashes in the provinces. BJ Habibie, Soeharto's crony vice president, wandered mindlessly through the ruins, giggling at the incredulity of his sudden elevation to the presidency. This was followed by a more orderly transition based on the general elections of 1999. The election was a first for Indonesia, apparently fair and open involving over ninety million voters and forty-eight political parties. Even Jimmy Carter gave his imprimatur on the orderliness of the democratic event. Of course a nice man like Carter had no inkling that Soeharto's electoral machinations were not that easily abandoned by the Golkar politicians who had thirty years experience in raising and using illicit funds. They elected enough people of the past to make it impossible for a man like Gus Dur to function as a president. A nearly blind religious intellectual, he had been written off by almost everyone as too frail to serve. But frailness was not his problem. In fact, he became too robust in his drive for reform that the dark forces of the past soon realized that they had to stop him by whatever means necessary.

In 1998 it was quite simple to say that we did not want Soeharto and we wanted to work for reform. The Soeharto people were in the government, the reformers were outside. As we moved from the Habibie to Wahid administrations it became more difficult to carry out reform. It should have been done by a combination of pressure from the outside with the best effort on the inside. But with suspicion being spread by the media, those who remained outside saw people who joined the structure as being co-opted. Some good people on the inside, especially those who do not grow up with the reform movement, saw the activists outside as baggage??? trying to keep the government running. This climate of distrust would have been not be all that bad if it was not superimposed on the larger problem, which was that as the reformers tried to do their work, the old system was steadfast in resisting change. When reformers came into government during the Wahid presidency, the resistance to reform solidified.

In stark contrast, Megawati came to power not using the energy of *reformasi*, but by using the political vote in Parliament and the Assembly. It was heavily supported by big money mobilized by experienced operators. Megawati's ascendance also made use of the power of military and police, steering away from Gus Dur to a new system which actually turned out to be the old system with a new helmswoman at the wheel.

So we have come full circle from the heavy Soeharto regime to a lighter Habibie regime, to a wide-open Wahid-

Megawati regime and now back to a regime with New Order values. Soeharto actually remained in power after his resignation in 1998 and as this book goes to press he is still there. I am certain that if he were still president his cabinet would not be much different from the current Megawati cabinet.

Gus Dur, The Renaissance Man

Speaking as an independent commentator in Sydney in August 2000, I said that "Indonesia is conducting reform at a difficult time, under the bankruptcy of the legal, political, economic and leadership systems." Often when people undergo major surgery they can choose the best moment for the operation—that is when their bodies are fit and strong. Indonesia had no such luxury. Our legal system had never risen back to the levels of the Dutch days, our banks had collapsed, our military had discredited itself. All the institutions had collapsed, and the only institution that functioned in Indonesia in the last thirty-some years was Soeharto. In this chaotic and destroyed state, plans are difficult to implement. The state was rotting away, the government was not functioning and people felt there was very little hope.

The figure of Gus Dur was a major source of hope for reform. He is the one person in Indonesia we can count on to advocate and to defend the core values of pluralism, diversity and ethnic tolerance. He not only believes in these things, but he actually goes so far as to send people to defend churches and minorities.

President Wahid was conducting social reform ahead of bureaucratic reform. In his presidency he has repealed several laws aimed against ethnic Chinese. Visible signs of this historic reform still abound. Chinese New

Year is once more openly celebrated. Chinese characters adorn signs in Indonesian cities and a television station broadcasts news in the Chinese language. However, some Chinese equal rights group still complain that Indonesia's bureaucracy continues to discriminate against them on many levels. It gave me pride that President Wahid had the determination to invite members of the nation's ethnic Chinese minority to use their traditional Chinese names some thirty years after they were regulated into adopting Indonesian-sounding ones. Former President Soeharto forced hundreds of thousands of ethnic Chinese families to take on indigenous names in a campaign of assimilation.

A true intellectual, Gus Dur speaks five languages including Javanese. He used to read, when his eyesight was better, French novels in French, Dutch novels in Dutch, German novels in German and Russian novels in the English translation. He knows the books of Karl Marx almost as well as he does the Koran. He likes to outwit people. He took delight in outwitting Soeharto, Habibie, Wiranto and he even outwits his own supporters. He overcame the *interpelasi* (censure) motion of Parliament in August 2000 but the belligerence of the parliamentarians would go on, prodded by the media and fuelled by political money.

The high hopes placed on the Wahid presidency were the reason for deep public disappointment when his government faltered in the face of strong political headwinds. Disappointment started even when President Wahid announced his first cabinet. The choice of cabinet ministers was a product of appeasement to the coalition that had elected him. Many were second-rate choices in terms of competence. Gus Dur did not even know many of them. When people complained about one cabinet minister, Gus Dur said, "Why complain to me? He was put there by (Golkar party chief) Akbar Tandjung. I don't even know the guy." He said that as a joke, which I thought was very funny. He kept telling jokes which we thought were funny until we realized that the economy was not going anywhere and that the economy isn't something you can cure with jokes.

It is true, however, that difficult political matters could be resolved by expert application of wits. The way he dismissed (former military chief) General Wiranto was a classic example of sophisticated political juggling. People do not quite remember now that at that point Wiranto was very strong. The way President Wahid danced around like Mohammed Ali, taking verbal pot-shots at General Wiranto from one capital to another as he was on a European tour, was unique. It was a method tailor-made to deal with Wiranto who is not geared to trade soundbites. It also was a demonstration of knowing the enemy as well as knowing the field. As a tactician Gus Dur is masterful. His weakness, as Professor Daniel Lev of the University of Washington has pointed out, is that Gus Dur was a president acting without the institutions of government. He faced resistance from Soeharto's New Order in the form of provocation in the provinces and in sensitive trouble spots. Gus Dur was bereft of the strength a president needed to confront them. The money, the weapons, the networks were not in Gus Dur's hands. He had the tacit support of intellectuals, students and of course his mass base at NU. But they were not politically mobilized and were no match for the highly trained political-money-military machine of Soeharto.

Gus Dur was the victim of over-expectation, media hype and loss of public perspective. Take the Bulogate scandal, in which Gus Dur's private masseur used his name to extract money from Bulog (the state logistics agency). Even now, we don't know what the facts of the matter are except that Gus Dur neither planned the scam nor gained anything from the shenanigans. The money involved was equivalent to US$4.1 million. That stands in stark contrast to the to US$110 million involved in the Bank Bali scandal attributed to the Golkar party in President Habibie's time, a corruption case which up till the present day has not been resolved. Soeharto siphoned off something in the order of US$15 billion from state funds over his three decades of power. These scandals were never reported by the Indonesian press for thirty-two years. The schemes were very carefully planned, very carefully executed and they were huge. Habibie's scandals are smaller, well planned but rather carelessly executed, so that they were revealed in the press. Gus Dur's alleged scandals—which remain to this day nothing more than allegations—were totally unplanned, unorchestrated and the sums involved were comparatively very, very small.

Clearly Gus Dur's people should have convinced him right from the very beginning of the necessity and the power of public communications. He never had an effective public relations operation. He doesn't believe in managing the press, which is a good thing but can be counter-productive. He just goes out and does things, and it was a tragedy to the nation that people exploited that weakness as his supporters failed to shore up his support system. As Indonesian citizens we should take matters into our own hands by insisting on accountable behavior and on good governance, rather than focusing on a single person. There were many who shared this opinion. In fact, it might have been the reason I was invited on board. But by that time it had turned out to be an impossible task, as the political rot had set in. The Wahid presidency was put on the top of the hit list of very aggressive politicians who cut short Indonesia's journey into humanism and democracy. By the time I joined, the problem was no longer public relations but political sabotage. Maybe I was miscast as the person charged to rescue the presidential image, but in terms of willingness to do the job I had the psychological fit. I would do anything as long as I believed in it.

Not Really a Submarine Cook

As Gus Dur walked the earth to listen and spread the word, I went through several changes of life in much more mundane settings: high school student in middle-class Jakarta, going off to study at the Bandung Institute of Technology (ITB), socializing in student organizations, going off to the States to unsuccessfully finish my education, until circumstances brought me to do more interesting things. Suddenly Peter Waldman described me as the 'avatar of this country's emboldened radical chic' in a *Wall Street Journal* profile. I had to look up the word *avatar* and I will let you figure that one out yourself too, but the point is that I ended up doing many different things in my fifty-six years. Most of my interesting roles have come almost by accident, so that my kids have come to call me 'the Forrest Gump of Indonesia.'

When I was a little boy, my brother Rachmat used to tell me stories. They were very entertaining, sometimes quite inspiring. It doesn't matter that most of his stories turned out to be totally untrue. For instance, he told me that *Bang* Mis'an, the man who painted our house, also painted the sky. As the house-painter was a very nice man, it made me look up to him more, and the more you look up to people the more comfortable you are. So that was an untruth which proved to be beneficial to me. Sometimes we would pass the church opposite Gambir station which had a cupola, a little glass dome on top of the roof. I would wonder what it was for, and my brother, never at a loss for an answer, told me that's where naughty boys got sent for punishment. I asked, "How come I never see anyone there?" He said, "They only get put up there at night, since it's not scary in the daytime." That really scared me, and for many years I would drop off into silence whenever I passed that building.

I found these stories to be sometimes useful but always entertaining. One useless but charming piece of misinformation I got was that cows in Argentina had flesh with the texture of corned beef. That is why we get our canned corned beef from Argentina. I borrowed from my brother's art and continued the tradition, telling tales to my sons when they where little. Their favorite topic was a world made of foodstuffs: roads made from chocolate, rivers flowing with soup, cars with doughnut wheels. But that is for another book. My kids liked to be told what kind of work I had done. They thought I was somebody who had done a lot of interesting things. Actually I just did a little bit of this and a little bit of that. I told them that I was once a football player, but could not make it into the big leagues because I was overweight and wore glasses. There was some truth as well as a lot of wistfulness there. I said I had been a driver for public transport—which I actually was for about two months—driving my father's three-wheeled *bemo*. I also told them I had been a high school teacher, taught English and Dutch to Indonesian housewives, algebra to teenage girls and piano to little kids—all true stories. Then I exaggerated. I said I had been a short-order cook in a submarine. That one really impressed my kids. At first they did not believe me and I was caught out on a limb, but I thought I would play it along some more. After a while they were sort of torn between belief and disbelief. It took great sensitivity to extricate myself from that bit of false representation.

By now they know that I had never been in a submarine except the time we did it together in Disneyland. I had also never been a short-order cook, let alone a combination of the two. But my career has been very haphazard and exciting. It has been fun. In my serious life I was a university lecturer, a management consultant and a real estate developer. Now people know me from television and radio and the printed press. In fact, in a bit of well-intended hyperbole Andrew Dodd wrote in a 13 July 2000 profile titled "A well-connected pundit" for the *Australian*: "His chubby features have become the international face of Indonesia. Audiences from London to New York have seen him almost bursting from their TV screens, quipping and joking and trying to make sense of the latest twists and turns in Indonesian affairs. In Indonesia, Witoelar is a household name."

I never took this kind of publicity too seriously, although I realize I am doing serious work. In the heyday of the creative American TV Series "The Simpsons" there was an episode in which Bart Simpson, the bratty young son, received instant fame for the delivery of a single line. He said, "I didn't do it," when the stage curtains in his school auditorium collapsed during an important school play. Bart had nothing to do with the disaster but his

A well-connected pundit

Having survived years of media oppression in Indonesia, Wimar Witoelar is enjoying democracy, writes **Andrew Dodd**

I can't resist showing off this very friendly profile in the Australian.
What did I do to deserve this kind treatment from the Australian press?

instinctive plaintive cry: "I didn't do it," hit the funny bone
of the public so squarely that he was invited to every TV
and radio show to repeat the line. Then, as Andy Warhol
observed, his fifteen minutes were up and he disappeared
into oblivion. My fifteen minutes have been longer—if not
as spectacular—than those of Bart Simpson. My days as a
student activist in 1966 had propelled me into prominence.
While others did the physically dangerous stuff of going
against Soekarno's government and dealing with
Soeharto's army, I instead did the talking in public rallies,
speaking in forums, and writing articles in newspapers.

∽∾

It is interesting that President Soekarno has been
rehabilitated in our sense of history by the majority of
Indonesians, while I was politically born in the anti-

Soekarno student movement in 1966. Now I neither support Soeharto nor condemn the Communists of Indonesia, a reversal of my public attitude back in the sixties. You can attribute that to youth, misinformation or some other excuse. But I think there is a more substantial attitude at work here, and it is important to draw it out to understand the political bias of this book. While the emotions of the student and mass movements of 1966 represented anti-Communism, mine represented anti-totalitarianism. I admired Soekarno when he was dreaming of a new world order, but I disliked his anti-democratic actions in the last years of his rule leading to 1965.

We rejected the international communist bloc in favor of the 'free world' led by the United States, but I was turned off by US political conservatism even in the sixties, quickly identifying myself with the American political Left to the extent that I could understand them. Richard Nixon, Ronald Reagan and George Bush (both of them) were never my heroes. JFK, George McGovern and Jimmy Carter were people I trusted.

My student activism led to exciting public experiences and an active role in student politics. I was a national-level student leader and had a respectable term as student council president of ITB. ITB is Indonesia's oldest engineering school which we liked to describe at that time as the 'MIT of Indonesia'. Aside from a good academic reputation, its students have played a substantial political role in the nation. My political career was cut short when a stay in America during the early seventies changed my public outlook. My political ambitions were quelled as I realized we had unwittingly escorted the country into the grip of a very strong, corrupt and ruthless regime—Soeharto's New Order.

Back in Bandung as university lecturer at ITB in 1975 after four years studying in the United States, I closed myself off from formal politics. I tried to be a model faculty member but occasionally hung around with the student leaders of that period. Unfortunately, even this hanging around brought the weight of the regime down on me. The 1978 General Session of the Assembly was approaching when Bandung students started demonstrating against the reelection of Soeharto, more a statement than reflecting any degree of reality.

Things really heated up when the students went on strike and refused to listen to the university administration. Tanks rolled in from the crack Siliwangi division and troops occupied the ITB campus for a few weeks. Hundreds of students were detained and released after a few days, but I was held for almost a month as I was a faculty member who was accused of exhorting the students to rebel. After Soeharto was reelected we were all released without any formal decision, as the arrest was also made without formal charges. That was the New Order power game. Although the student movement was unsuccessful it was a good exercise in political mobilization. Many of the student leaders of that '1978 generation' are now in the top levels of the executive and legislative branches of government. The earlier '1966 generation' are now receding into history as they had a satisfying run in government and politics with Soeharto until 1998, while the 'Last of the Mohicans' like Akbar Tandjung are now clinging on for their political lives.

In the eighties when I was living the quiet life of a management consultant my best friend and fellow student activist Sarwono Kusumaatmadja, who was at the time a

As young faculty member at ITB in Bandung, I supported student calls asking President Soeharto to step down. Being at the height of his power, Soeharto flicked away the movement without missing a beat at the People's Consultative Assembly in 1978. I got a month in detention.

cabinet minister in Soeharto's government, said in a magazine interview: "Wimar's career peak came when he was student council president of ITB in 1969. After that it has been downhill," a typical example of Sarwono's sharp humor which I appreciated. But true fame (without the fortune) started in 1993 when I was suddenly pushed into the public eye because of my *Perspektif* television talk show. It brought me instant public recognition, especially when the Soeharto regime banned the show. We happened to react to the censure in a different way, not openly rebelling but maintaining our position. That brought a lot of supporters to our side. In fact, our public profile became much stronger after the banning.

The difference in our reaction was that we neither capitulated by disappearing from the scene, nor did we oppose the decision in a hard-line political way, which would have scared off people. We just found the humor in the banning and moved the television show to the stage. Instead of having a *Perspektif* television talk show, we had a *Perspektif Live!* stage show which we would hold in hotels around Jakarta and eventually around the country. People liked the spirit of the events. They could see live what they used to watch on television. My producer Hani Hasyim expertly re-created a genuine *Perspektif* ambience by making the stage look like a TV set. Occasionally we used a large screen monitor, so people could look at the screen and pretend they were watching a television show.

More than that, Hani and the crew at InterMatrix, our small company, maintained a tongue-in-cheek presence. It was natural to keep a humorous manner, one in fact bordering on self-parody because we also sold T-shirts, bags, caps—all kinds of mementos of the show. It also commercialized our ideas, at least in style if not in amounts of money. When somebody accused me of commercializing democracy I said, "Sure, but it's better than commercializing tyranny." I like to think that it was snappy remarks like that which made the public comfortable with us.

Based on the *Perspektif Live!* show we were invited to do radio shows and contribute newspaper columns, and then magazine columns and content to news portals. We also published a monthly magazine ourselves entitled *Indonesian Business*. So in about seven years, from 1993 to 2000, we had managed to transform our small management consulting company into a respectably-sized media company.

The point of this story is to bring out my background, to help you understand the spirit in which this book is written. It is really a 'worm's-eye' view as well as a 'bird's-eye' view, a look at life as I saw it, constantly changing angles like a photographer changes lenses, to find the best perspectives. I have always liked the media, always felt comfortable with them and I have never regretted my association with the press. Outsiders saw the media treatment of President Wahid as being unfair or biased. This judgment is undoubtedly true, but I think the heart of the media is still with us, as people against corruption and violence. I suspect that some media people were and are compromised by money and by pressure from political groups. Some are helping to maintain a system that is unkind to the people. The media is also a subject of the system. The power system and the money system is not operated by angels. I will leave moral judgment on the media to other occasions. Here I just wish to point out that were it not for the media, we would not be where we are now in Indonesia, for better or for worse.

My actual entry into media was accidental and informal. One morning in late 1993 Djoko Soemantri, an executive of SCTV, then a new television station in Jakarta, invited me for a business breakfast. The topic was corporate restructuring and improving company perform- ance at SCTV. InterMatrix, the management consulting company I founded and ran, had completed several successful projects in these areas. SCTV was interested, but I was not because of my heavy work load at that time. "If you want your station to be recognized it must have a signature show," I said, "like a different kind of talk show." Djoko was interested. They talked about talk shows, and then Djoko asked, "But who could do it?" I replied by reflex, "Me," because I had done this kind of thing before in my days as graduate student in the United States twenty years before. Djoko suggested a one-page proposal and set up a meeting for me with Steve Mathis, a flamboyant

Hollywood type with decades of experience as a talk show producer who also was the senior programming adviser at SCTV. Steve gave me a chance for a pilot without a screen test. "I know a talk show host when I see one," he said. The rest, as they say, is history. The *Perspektif* show was an instant hit and its sequel, *Selayang Pandang* on Indosiar TV station won me prizes three years in a row from Indonesian national television's prestigious Panasonic Awards, twice as Best Male Talk Show Host.

Crossing Paths

So there we were, the great man and I, meeting at the crossroads of history. Gus Dur and I come from very different backgrounds and our levels of activism were as different as heaven and earth.

But we were brought together because of many things. Most directly the reform movement brought us together. In the Soeharto times, ordinary citizens were isolated from public discussion. You either had to be part of the Golkar-dominated formal political system or have very special strengths. Gus Dur possessed special strength by his own merit and as leader of a mass organization tens of millions strong. No matter what official position he might or might not occupy, Gus Dur was always a factor in Indonesian politics. When Gus Dur was up for chairmanship of NU, the Soeharto power center tried in vain to prevent it. In turn, Gus Dur did not push his luck and moved NU out of the political arena. His agility in dealing for a peaceful coexistence with the Soeharto power center while remaining a moral beacon made him a figure I admired from afar.

The distance between Gus Dur's political tradition and mine seemed so great that I felt flattered when he engaged me in a serious discussion on politics during a chance encounter in an airport in 1996. However, that was not our first meeting. The very first one was on a television recording session for my *Perspektif* talk show at the YTC studio near the Ragunan Zoo. It was 1994 approaching the World Cup in the United States. Gus Dur had always been a soccer fan and he was doing World Cup soccer analysis for *Kompas* newspaper. Since the government censors would never allow the broadcast of a political discussion with Gus Dur, I decided to approach him from the soccer angle. To my pleasure he responded beautifully, drawing subtle metaphors to bring across some very strong political points. There were enough tantalizing illustrations of defensive play, long passes, feigned movements and goalkeeper blunders to make the conversation interesting both from the straight soccer perspective as well as from the political innuendo. It was my first direct encounter with the famous wit and wisdom of Gus Dur. When we met again at the airport I not only managed to

Meeting Gus Dur on the same flight to Solo in 1996, I grabbed a chance to have my picture taken with this great man I only knew from far away.

have our picture taken but established the rapport I had with him.

As I felt I was an ordinary man who did not belong in the high altitudes of politics and moral movements, I never thought of Gus Dur as somebody with whom I would have more than chance encounters. But nobody expected the tremendous social upheaval that came with the rapid decline and fall of the New Order. The wheel of history turned and Gus Dur's group, who had been at the lower end of the political order, suddenly found themselves sharing the top spot with the Megawati nationalists and urban middle class. It was more a case of popular sentiment, especially well-articulated by the student and pro-democracy movement, pushing the cart and turning the wheel than the wheel turning by its own source of power. In any case the political order had reversed in 1998 and Soeharto's crowd were cowering in the dark corners as the forces of reform paraded around feeling the suddenly clean political air.

A political vacuum was created and people like me were sucked into it. No longer needing the legitimacy of the Soeharto-cum-Golkar institutions, the ordinary people were able to articulate and empower themselves on the basis of their own convictions. The little niche I had carved out for myself in the world of political discourse turned into a thriving platform of public discourse. Like the lone prospector poking around rocks out of habit, I suddenly found a rich lode of gold in the form of people with whom we could communicate as equals. Human rights activists, legal reformers, idealistic economists, gender advocates, moral leaders all converged in the new political elite. To be sure, the old guard was still there, lurking silently and watching their stashes of power and money. As it turned out later, they might yet resurrect their corrupt order. But for a while, optimism ruled the day.

It was in this environment that I crossed paths with Gus Dur. Change is always a democratizing agent, and his casual attitude in the climate of transition broke down the huge distance in our statures even further. I was able to join him because I never felt too small to matter in a new world in which everybody was welcome. The actual process of recruitment was as strange as it was typical of Gus Dur.

PART TWO

ON THE ROLLERCOASTER

The Day My Nap Was Interrupted

I remember it was a Sunday in September 2000. Sunday has always been my favorite day for an afternoon nap. I was interrupted by a telephone call from a reporter, which was normal. This time it was from detik.com, the primary news portal of Indonesia. But the question was totally unexpected.

The reporter asked, "*Bang* Wimar, are you going to accept your appointment as the Presidential Spokesman?" I said, "What kind of joke is this? What do you mean?" "Well, haven't you heard? It was just published on our website. President Abdurrahman Wahid has nominated you to be the Presidential Spokesman." I replied, "I can't respond to that. I haven't even heard the news myself." I hung up and immediately logged onto the internet. Sure enough, there it was in the detik.com news portal: in a speech in Medan, President Wahid announced that he was going to appoint five spokesmen, and I was to be the chief.

Later on I received several similar calls from the press. I had to respond in a more specific way. So I explained, "Well, if it *is* true then it is indeed a rare privilege. Of course, I have to think about it and consult my family and my friends in my business, because of course it's a big decision." I then called several people who were close to Gus Dur. The only such persons I knew were Yenny Wahid, his daughter, and Dr. Greg Barton, an Australian academic who is Gus Dur's biographer. Yenny had been a reporter for the *Sydney Morning Herald* and Greg is a professor from Deakin University in Melbourne whom I had met on my visits to Australia. He has been close to Gus Dur for many years and in the last few years was constantly at his side. Greg had been in Jakarta the previous month and I met him and Yenny a few times. They both confirmed that President Wahid had mentioned my name on several occasions, and that it was true that he wanted me for the to-be-created position of chief presidential spokesman.

I consulted no one but my family. I was leaning towards acceptance, and I knew my family would be supportive. Everybody in my immediate family has substantial sympathy for Gus Dur's persona and political character. They more or less agreed I should accept the offer, providing the terms of work supported this special assignment. I did not bother to contact others. Somehow I felt that this was a very personal decision and I feared that others would be more inclined to point out the forbidding risk-to-reward outlook in the proposition.

Many asked me if I did not feel I was giving away too much accepting this thankless position. I never saw it that way. I felt it was an opportunity of a lifetime to do something for others. I had always been working on my own, doing things for myself. Now I felt I was needed. Being in the front row of the audience watching political history was something I had always wanted. I did not have many doubts accepting the challenge. Many people did have reservations but not my family—my wife and my children were very supportive. We are a close-knit family, starting from my parents and their one daughter and four sons, of whom I am the youngest. I have always felt my parents are the most successful ones in the world because we were so close as a family. I have always had the benefit of my elders' guidance, from the days when brother Toerki would not let me eat ice cream in the family car because I had spilled it once. Besides imposing discipline, he supported me significantly through life by providing material support and encouraging precision and productivity.

My eldest brother Luki is almost my spiritual and emotional twin, and was cautiously enthusiastic about the president's offer, with the same excitement and apprehension I was feeling. I did not ask the opinion of Rachmat, my closest brother, because I knew what he would say. He is the rational and pragmatic one, and this was not a time to be practical. In fact I stayed away from people who were my longtime political advisors, because if I were to respond to Gus Dur's offer it would have to be with a totally fresh outlook on life. I had unwittingly experienced a generational change by moving from a New Order student leader to a nineties media person. My world were the twenty-somethings and thirty-somethings in my company, my TV shows, the movement and the press. It was the time to listen to Greg, who gave strong intellectual comfort, and to Yenny, who gave me ample emotional grounds to trust the first family of the country at that time.

I believed in Gus Dur because he is in many ways a refreshing figure on the Indonesian political landscape. For thirty years I had observed political life in Indonesia where leadership was insincere, corrupt, violent and deceitful. And here comes a person who seemed to be sincere, and being attacked politically, misunderstood by the public and abandoned by many good people. I thought if all the good people left him, he would end up having nobody. So I thought I should just jump in and help him for as long as it would take. I thought that even if my contribution was not to prove successful, at least I would have had the satisfaction of trying. I would have felt guilty had I simply stayed at home watching him being attacked.

My colleagues, friends, workplace partners had doubts about the job because I had a nice little thing going at work, doing a lot of shows, constantly appearing in public, making some money. My fans enjoyed my freewheeling style and were worried about losing me on TV and radio. But these drawbacks paled in significance compared to the massive adventure ahead of me. I knew it could be a losing game, but being invited to defend your country in its greatest hour of need has a special kind of appeal, a once-only offer I could not refuse. Closing my ears to any other advice I went to Marsillam Simandjuntak, a longtime friend and one of very few persons in political life who has never eroded the hundred percent trust I quietly gave him. He was the cabinet secretary and it was his job to prepare the legalities of presidential appointments. Making sure I knew what I was doing, Marsillam started to draw up the presidential decree for my appointment. But I still had to see the president and ask him what he really wanted of me. So I asked for a meeting.

The president's aide asked me to come during the president's private hour—5:30 in the morning— and I could accompany him on his walk around the palace and have a chat.

I made it to the palace at the appointed time, even after spending some time finding out which gate to enter. I had never been into the palace before until that day, short of two brief visits: once in 1969, when General H.R. Dharsono was installed as Ambassador to Thailand, and then in 1993 when my brother Rachmat was installed as Ambassador to Russia. Those were the only two times I had been in the palace. And the third time was then, to talk to the president about a job at the presidential office.

He didn't say anything when I came except, "Oh, *Pak* Wimar!" He had already started on his rounds, and continued his conversation as I joined the two or three people on the morning walk. I forced myself to relax as I walked at his side and chatted about political issues. I asked him about Bulogate. I asked him about Suwondo, the masseur who used his name to get the illegal funds. I asked him about a lot of things where I had doubts, because I thought before I joined him I had to be sure that he was clean. But it wasn't an intensive interrogation, just a casual talk.

He is a very informal man, and as such there were no contract negotiations. We just spoke about our political ideas and what sort of freedom I would have as his spokesman. I did have lots of freedom. In fact he never instructed me to do anything. I was there to find my own way and support him to the best of my abilities.

We walked around for another hour and we sat down. So I said, what would the role of the chief spokesman entail and what was I expected to do? Well, the president said, you're a good communicator. You don't need to interpret me so much as to provide the press with background and context to the issues. I thought to myself, that makes sense as President Wahid operated with a high degree of sophistication in dialogue. Say if he talked about the Middle East or ASEAN, many people wouldn't know enough background to follow his thinking intelligently. It is as of he were a professor and he needed a teaching assistant to supply students with additional data, additional background material.

So I thought, "Ah, that's my job, that's good!" Could I come to him, ask him to clarify things to me? He said, sure. What are the terms of access? Oh, anytime. With those words I was given unlimited access to the president. I did not use it most of the time, because I didn't want to bite off more than I could chew. I didn't involve myself in his private affairs either—just limiting myself to presidential business. I thought these were very good terms of work.

I worked closely with my old friend Marsillam, the cabinet secretary. I asked him if he could show me the ropes. First I had to learn how to get in and out of the Presidential Palace. The president might *say* that I had unlimited access, but the guards did not necessarily know that. We were required to wear a tiny lapel pin as a form of ID—which I made a mental note to get sorted out right away. I asked Marsillam about some other logistical matters, but he just said, "You're only responsible to the president, so make your own place. Nobody can touch you." That sounded reasonable, so I found my own way around.

By that time President Wahid had already dismayed many of his supporters and confounded most of his political rivals, showing himself to be difficult to understand. He was dynamic in the eyes of his supporters and wishy-washy in the eyes of his opponents, but I never thought he lacked consistency. Just as you cannot judge Giuseppe Verdi on the basis of a single musical phrase, you cannot judge Gus Dur on the basis of a single statement. I always felt that Gus Dur was continuously making technical adjustments to face a very uncertain and hostile environment. And I had always felt that Gus Dur is first and foremost a man of wisdom and a man of peace, as substantiated by his twenty-year long track record. I also knew that he was basically a proponent of gradual evolutionary change, as Greg Barton would say, rather than an advocate of radical revolution or sudden change.

Parliamentary Lashing

First day at work, October 8. I had just been introduced to Dr. Indrawadi Tamin who was coordinating logistics for the spokesmen. Indrawadi was the deputy presidential secretary in charge of press and protocol. A smooth, intelligent man, Indrawadi showed me around the office, provided me with the necessary working logistics. Substance was not discussed as that was between the president and me, but household items were, and these were very important. First, I asked him for an office and he showed me several options and I took the first one I saw.

The position of spokesman was freshly created, never having existed either in the Wahid administration nor in any of the preceding ones. While looking at the office I was also measured for a suit. Turns out we got one suit made and paid for by the government. Still nobody knew about salary arrangements so I decided to have someone else look into it. After a few weeks they found the government salary allotment which was a whopping two million rupiah (around US$200 at that time) plus gasoline coupons for two hundred liters a month. I flinched at the small amount but there was no complaint inside me, just amusement, because I had resolved to see the job as a privilege rather than a career step.

The next item on the list was the lapel pin. This is the most important piece of equipment—as it must be worn to gain access around the Presidential Palace. They come in different colors and mine was red. I asked a security officer what the colors meant and he said, "Well, let me put it this way. Green gets you inside the grounds, blue gets you inside the presidential offices, but with your pin color you have access right to the president's nose." I thought that was pretty clear and made up for the low pay.

Later that morning I was notified by Indrawadi that a delegation from Parliament would meet the president at the State Palace, which is the part of the Presidential Palace complex used for public official functions. So I went along with him, new boy in school, and I was quite thrilled to see all the cabinet ministers, the armed forces commanders, the one hundred parliamentary leaders, and the president and vice president all together in one room. We sat with a high level of decorum. The main hall was split into two sides along the length of the room. On the west side you have the parliamentary delegations, headed by Chairman Akbar Tandjung and his Deputy Chairman AM Fatwa. Fatwa represented the Reform Faction—the political base of Amien Rais. On the east side of the room you had the president, vice president, and his cabinet. Susilo Bambang Yudhoyono, the coordinating minister for political and social affairs, was there as well as a number of key ministers. They were joined by the heads of the armed forces and Chief of Police Bimantoro, who had just

The president, vice president and major cabinet members lined up for a dialogue with parliamentary leaders which turned out to be a diatribe by one of the politicians. Tough for me, sitting in the back on my first day at work.

been installed. I was sitting in the second row, which I came to learn would be my regular place, one rank below the president and the cabinet ministers who were in the front row.

As a social event it was interesting because I shook hands with everybody there. They welcomed me to my new position, and many of them I had known from previous contact in our public lives. Some of them, as in the case of military commanders, were quite new. I met Police Bimantoro in the toilet and he said that he liked my TV show. A lot of people said the same thing, so there was some satisfaction that people actually *did* watch the show.

Fatwa, who was going to be a main figure in this little drama, also met me. With a strange kind of cordial skepticism, he said, "Well, I am glad you are on board, I hope you can put some sense into President Wahid's public statements." But a bit later during his tirade he changed the angle: "First we have a buffoon as a president. Then when we thought he would shape up, he hires another buffoon as his spokesman."

If Fatwa was the bad guy in the meeting, Akbar Tandjung was the good guy. He was his usual self: polite, non-committal, seemingly neutral and generally a soothing influence. Gus Dur responded in usual fashion: with good nature, fatherly and with a touch of light humor. Megawati as ever smiled her famous smile and did her famous act of silence. The cabinet ministers were on standby, looking ahead to a day of discourse between the top levels of the government's executive and legislative branch. After the opening, Fatwa took over and what he said sent chills up my spine which I still feel to this very day. It was not just that he went into a barrage of attacks on President Wahid right from the beginning. Political attacks have been my staple for thirty years, acrimony is the spice of life in politics. But what really struck me was the viciousness and rudeness of a scale I had never before witnessed. It made the entire scene unpalatable.

As the meeting was off-limits to the press, the public are not aware of the level of discourtesy that was demonstrated here. Transcripts have been circulated, so at least people can see the content. There was not much content in the speech by Fatwa. His theme was that the president was not only guilty of incompetence and ill intention, but that he was actually incapable to function because of a poor mental state. He accused the president of being erratic and psychologically unsound, and went so far as to say that the president told lies and probably had not recovered from his stroke.

Being new in this room full of big names, I was not aroused to hostility, but instead felt waves of sadness and disappointment that the people whom the public had entrusted to build a new political culture were so callous in applying the power they had so recently gained. Their positions were gained through the effort and sacrifices made by students and the civil society. Now they are lashing out with no civility at a president who was trying to do what he is supposed to do. Many mistakes may be laid at the government's door, many mistakes have been made by the president as a human being, but I do not believe that there was incompetence to a degree which could justify Fatwa's remarks. In fact, Fatwa's attack was so unjustified that to his credit Akbar Tandjung apologized for them later on. Several parliament leaders in fact walked out of the hall where the meeting was being held. Some I met in the toilet and just shook their head or indicated to me that this is not their language. Of course they could not commit themselves any more than that. I had not necessarily hoped for kindness from the parliament for a president that I know they are not supporting, but I had hoped for a minimum level of decency that one expects from a statesman, or even a politician at this high level.

The attacks went on and on until Akbar Tandjung intervened. I could see Susilo Bambang Yudhoyono being very uncomfortable looking at the president and the vice president. Even Megawati said later on in a conversation that she even heard Susilo Bambang Yudhoyono grinding his teeth together to keep his cool. Megawati herself was very sympathetic to Gus Dur. She kept giving him comforting pats on the hand, providing mints, water and tissue to calm him down. Actually the only calm person in that room was President Wahid himself. When his time came to reply he did not counterattack Fatwa. He just acknowledged the comments politely and was succinctly responsive in his answer.

The meeting ended without much more excitement because Akbar Tandjung cut it short, and the issues in fact never got resolved. Actually, I was quite impressed on that first day at work to witness President Wahid's performance at that meeting. While he ignored Fatwa's attack, he did respond to the ten written questions Parliament had prepared. Gus Dur replied verbally, as always, as his loss of eyesight means that he cannot read. What was amazing to me was not just the quality of the replies, which more or less covered the issues, but the fact that he could recite them all from memory. They were ten quite technical issues, ranging from legislative action to security policies and all-encompassing economic policies. All ten issues were presented in a form that was lost in the attack by Fatwa.

The next day, on our morning walk, I told Gus Dur I was really trembling at that meeting. I thought that meeting was really disappointing, that I felt I could not go on hearing this type of nasty talk by a parliament leader, vitriolic language devoid of content. Gus Dur just said

*Gus Dur started work at 5 o'clock receiving people,
and by 6:30 we would have a breakfast briefing, this time with
Foreign Minister Alwi Shihab and Hasan Wirayudha.*

"Wimar, why don't you just relax, Fatwa is like that. Those people are like that, why should we worry? We just do our thing, and we should not be tempted because if we get angry then we will be dragged down to their level." That was very soothing, and Gus Dur never displayed any public anger. However, much later he did put his foot down officially. He said he would no longer accept such parliamentary delegations since they are not compulsory, unless the parliament leadership guaranteed that they would refrain from using improper language. That remark met with counter-remark which led to nowhere. Ever since that unpleasant day the forum of a hundred leading parliamentarians and the president was never held again.

Guests in the Palace

The dramatic first day at work set the standard for the highs and the lows of my time with Gus Dur. But it does not tell the story of the Wahid presidency. His presidency is most of all about a house open to the people, a political office made available by a president who was the ultimate 'people person'. This was the strength and the weakness of the Wahid presidency. It was apparent from the first day at work that our days would be constantly filled by people coming and going. Many times I would not know the exact identities of the people milling around the president, even less what they were up to behind the topics they had come to discuss. Having always been involved with people, including watching politics operate through friends who had become politicians and public officials, I am fully aware of the maelstrom of interests, subterfuge and opportunism revolving around positions of power.

President Wahid did apply some official rules of access to his office, but there were numerous occasions when people would be able to walk up to him without hinderance. Gus Dur's morning walks were always accompanied by three or four guests, sometimes even more. There were several ways to get invited to take part in these walks and permission was granted in a liberal fashion. Even people who were known to have dubious track records were occasionally admitted. When I questioned this, Gus Dur explained that it was good to know what these people had in mind. Usually they just came to chat and feel out the president. Things were rarely negotiated on a detailed basis in my presence but issues were often referred by the president to officials in charge for further follow-up. It is interesting to note that very few of these people who professed to enjoy early morning chats with Gus Dur didn't show up in the days after he was dismissed from office.

Other contact took place during the president's visits to various establishments. People would come up to Gus Dur or sit next to him and have serious conversations. The Friday prayers were famous for all kinds of people joining in the conversation afterwards. Gus Dur was adamant that his communication with the people should be maintained. Unfortunately this openness was often abused by the press, who would later take Gus Dur's informal and contextual comments and turn them into sensational, attention-grabbing headlines.

Whenever Gus Dur travels, he meets a lot of people because he feels that is the purpose of travel. He does not see any sense in going somewhere to officiate or give a formal speech without inviting feedback and if possible, conversation. When traveling abroad, the president always insisted that his time should be used to the fullest. That is why our schedules were inhumanely crowded whenever we visited a foreign country.

∼◦∼

Back in the palace, a normal working day consisted of meeting a stream of visitors. Around 4 o'clock each afternoon the presidential secretary would spend fifteen minutes with the president to discuss the next day's appointments. Each group of guests would be allotted thirty minutes, mostly in the president's private office within the palace's main building, but occasionally in the Bina Graha building where the formal offices were located. I had an office in the Bina Graha building but while in the palace I would just sit with the president by his desk in his office. I had a favorite chair which was hard and very comfortable for my bad back. Had things been different I would have asked for the chair as a going-away present.

We spokesmen were assigned rooms in Wisma Negara, the official guest house in the palace compound. They were like rooms in a 1970s three-star hotel: quite comfortable—if just a little seedy—with a TV and air-conditioning but the water was often not running, so we would have someone haul water in buckets to take showers. The main purpose of the room was to rest between work because our hours were long and irregular, sometimes starting at 4:30 with the morning walk and ending at 5:00 in the evening for me. The president often had an evening schedule which I only joined when the activities were public.

When people ask me if I really had a lot of power with such unlimited access my response would be in the negative. It is true the president allowed me to be with him all the time and gave me unrestricted access in the palace. I often used his private bathroom and watched

TV with his daughters, usually with a generous selection
of snacks. But my closeness was more due to the
generosity of the family's heart rather than my playing
any particular political role. Although dogs are rarely
used in positive metaphors in Indonesian culture, to some
people I would say that I was like a pet dog in the family.
I could walk in and out anywhere, be treated very nicely,
but that did not mean I had political power. Self-images
sometime pop up of myself as a White House dog, often
seen in pictures but not really influential in the councils
of state. In a kinder metaphor, I was John-John hiding
underneath JFK's desk.

The president's guests covered a broad spectrum. I
was not active in recommending visitors to the president
but I did help out by request to speed up appointments to
good people like human rights activists, civil society groups
and journalists (even though their articles were often very
critical of the president). One of the more satisfying visits
that I arranged was that of Angelique Widjaja and her
family. Angie was sixteen at that time and had just
astounded sports fans by winning the Wimbledon junior
singles title. Furthermore, she had done so without any
support from the state or from anyone outside her family.
I thought she would be an excellent role model for young
Indonesians and the president agreed. So we made a few
quick decisions and the next day she was at the palace,
charming everyone especially the press corps with her
candid and refreshing presence. She was one of the last
guests in the Wahid presidency. Earlier in my term I had
the good fortune to meet George McGovern who was the
Democratic Party's presidential candidate when I was
doing graduate studies in Washington, DC. I had
preferred him so much over the incumbent Richard Nixon

that I followed his campaign very closely. I told that to McGovern and had my picture taken like a schoolboy with his favorite Senator.

A surrealistic moment came when the president received Subandrio, Karim DP, and Ruslan Abdulgani with PDI-P eminence Amien Aryoso acting as the escort. Subandrio and friends were important figures in the Soekarno government when Soeharto took over power. Subandrio was even detained for many years after a military tribunal had sentenced him to death, a sentence which was commuted to life imprisonment and later release. They had come to request some humanitarian measures for themselves which President Wahid readily granted. The irony was that he assigned Marsillam Simandjuntak, who attended the meeting, to draw up the presidential decrees which would grant these requests. Marsillam had been a firebrand student leader when I was also active in the 1966 student movement. The students' major symbols of state

US Ambassador Robert Gelbard was controversial but the president liked him. With George McGovern, a favorite of mine, who came as a FAO official.

oppression and demonstration targets were precisely
Subandrio and his colleagues. Now he was instructed by
our president to administer mercy on behalf of the state.
The beauty of the situation was that we both agreed with
the president's decision. It was typical of Gus Dur's strong
conviction on mercy once justice had been served.

A memorable visit came from a group representing the
families of victims of state violence, students who were
killed in the 1998 shootings at Trisakti University and the
Semanggi I and Semanggi II incidents. They came with
human rights activists led by Karlina Leksono, a scientist
and housewife, who had emerged as one of the leaders of
our civil society. Theirs was a cause for justice and
compassion which had been very slow in eliciting support
from the government, both military and police. Their
exasperation peaked when Parliament, which had been
elected on the basis of their implied support of the student
movement, summarily dismissed their pleas and relegated
the case to the bleachers of the justice system. Only at the
presidential level did they finally meet with a solid
response. Unfortunately this president was to be replaced
a few weeks later by a new one, whose support the justice
seekers did not even dare to hope for.

So the guests came and went: the Henri Dunant
Foundation to request and approve extension of the peace
negotiations in Aceh, former IMF official Hubert Neiss
and New Order economic architect Widjojo Nitisastro,
scores of ambassadors and officials of foreign governments.
One time the president received Paul Dominguez, special
envoy of Philippine President Gloria Macapagal-Arroyo,
which was fun for me as Paul and I came to know each
other in 1969 when we were students organizing the first

ASEAUS, the Association of South-East Asian University Students. He had visited me in Bandung and I had even used his dormitory room and swimming pool when I visited Ateneo de Manila University where Dominguez was studying.

Cabinet ministers came and spent many interesting moments with the president, only a few of which are recounted in this book. But within the long list of visitors the president also received shysters and scoundrels, people fishing for position and favor and plain troublemakers who swarmed around the presidency like big flies around rich food.

We Talked About Ted Sorensen

Just as Gus Dur's fascinating human interaction over-shadowed the acrimony promoted in the press by an overzealous media, scandals and abusive language do not dominate the memories of my days with the president. Instead my memories will forever be colored by fond recollections of great conversations.

Gus Dur was never pretentious and never thought of anyone as being too important, not even himself. But he was able to enchant those around him with an uncanny insight built on volumes of wisdom and laced with humor. Just as great novels do not have to be about great themes, Gus Dur and I talked incessantly about any topic under the sun. Whenever others were not around we would expand to cover a very wide range, or shall I say, wild range, of subjects. From Beethoven to extreme radicalism, from medieval European history to internet technology. One of the favorite topics between the president and myself was American politics at the level of anecdotal history or even trivia. Gus Dur is the only man I know—except for

The President's daily briefings grew into a fascinating enlightening experience.

Luki my eldest brother—who has as much interest as myself in the little tidbits surrounding American political history, particularly of the fifties and sixties. That period was very thoroughly covered in the Western publications that managed to seep through to Indonesia, which at that time was experiencing tight censorship of the press. People like John F. Kennedy, Adlai F. Stevenson, Dwight D. Eisenhower, and even Barry Goldwater were different models of politicians who operated in open systems. The fact that they were human, and that their human activities were able to be covered in the public media, made following their activities more exciting than any soap opera.

We remembered in conversation a series of books written by Theodore White. The first one was *The Making of the President 1960*, which related to the JFK victory. This was of special interest because it was started in the Democratic primaries where the young junior senator from Massachusetts first made his mark. He had a press-friendly wife, Jacqueline Bouvier, and all the open competitors in a wide-open primary field, which JFK narrowly won. He ultimately mastered the Democratic Party in the convention in Los Angeles. Coming second at that time was Lyndon Johnson who eventually became his vice president. Gus Dur and I would talk about this. And we would talk about people like Theodore Sorensen, that young historian attached to the Kennedy staff and who now is one of the major American political history writers. Many know about John F. Kennedy, but only a few Indonesians I know have any idea who Ted Sorensen is. But we talked about Ted Sorensen and President Wahid would make the conversation interesting. Once in a while Gus Dur did talk about famous people like John F. Kennedy, and he would recite jokes that JFK told. One joke that I remember was this one: when Kennedy was in the Oval Office he would point at a little notch on the window sill behind his desk, and he would tell visitors with his unique brand of humor that the notch used to be Dwight D. Eisenhower's library, referring to the fact that President Eisenhower used to put his golf stick there.

Gus Dur liked the joke so much that he told the story to President Clinton to their mutual enjoyment when he visited him in the White House in 2000. The stories went on and on and on. Gus Dur had been given an audio book on Harry Truman by Yenny. Truman became his role model for a while, and maybe still is in a sense, because he is what Gus Dur is like: blunt, no nonsense, a wily politician, responsible, and best known for the sign that he put on his desk: "The Buck Stops Here."

What struck me at that time, while Gus Dur was able and willing to converse with me on topics of American historical trivia, was his superior knowledge in other aspects or areas of political history, say for instance the political history of the Middle East. Having lived in the Middle East for years as a student in Baghdad and Cairo and traveled extensively around the area, and of course being a Moslem cleric, he has a feel for the Middle East which I could never have. He knows the difference between the players in Iranian politics, and he told many amazing stories about Anwar Sadat and Hussein Mubarak. And he could talk with great authority on the Palestinian problem. To me he was a true Renaissance man.

The political discussions would extend to the present, where he talked about the politics in Taiwan and Malaysia, about the dynamics of the LDP, Japan's majority party. His erudition in history and politics came from reading, traveling and talking to a whole lot of people. There are stories that he would travel with suitcases filled with books. Throughout his life he developed huge networks of people. The persons that he followed through books later became people that he met in real life, and now he has become one of them.

Abdurrahman Wahid's lineage of larger-than-life people and his sense of destiny made it natural for him to weave in and out of the fabric of history as he spun his own contribution to Indonesian and world politics. I always had the feeling that his enthusiasm for story telling was not only based on his unusual memory for people and events but also his belief that these stories have messages to make our judgments better. It is as if he was creating templates of different scenarios from which we could select the most appropriate one for our needs. In that sense his practicality matches his intellectual framework. Even when we discussed religion he would not use the rostrum of undisputed religious authority, but use examples from the people in his stories. When he discussed a religion with me it was always with down-to-earth examples, probably because he knows my depth in religious knowledge is very modest. Talking religion with Gus Dur makes it all seem common sense and friendly. If people say he de-sanctified the presidency, to me he made religion non-threatening.

Otak-otak From Banten

Probably over time Gus Dur will himself become a historical figure of significant proportions. Certainly no greater person ever walked into my life. For me his greatness was enhanced by the abundance of human qualities which he brought into our lives. Never was a moment too serious to make us forget that we are individuals. Some small moments of great human significance are etched in my memory.

There were many domestic trips for the president in which I did not participate, mainly because there was an implicit understanding that domestic traveling would be divided among my two colleagues, Adhie Massardi and Yahya Staquf, and I would concentrate on international trips. One of the domestic trips was to the newly formed province of Banten which was adjacent to the capital region of Jakarta. The reason I didn't join this particular trip was that space was limited and the presidential tour would have to travel partly by helicopter to a remote area which was not possible to be reached by car. When they came back to the palace the next day, Vice President Megawati made some jokes as to why I was not part of the delegation. She said that the reason was because the helicopter had limited capacity and if I were to come along then I would have taken the place of three other people. This was all taken in good humor in one of the sessions of good cheer which often surrounded casual conversation with the vice president and the president. They then talked about some of the local delicacies they had a chance to sample on the trip, and I expressed disappointment that I missed this chance to expand my culinary horizon. It was a remark which I tossed off lightly in the spirit of the moment. That evening, after some lengthy conversations with the president and various guests, I set off for home. As usual I did not take leave from the president because he is not a man who stands on protocol.

Just as I arrived home a telephone call came from the president. He asked me where I was and I said I just arrived home. And he said, "Oh, that's too bad!" I said, "I'm sorry, do you want me to be at the palace? Is there still more work today?" He said, "Well, no, not really. But I thought if you were still in the palace grounds, I was going to give you some food we had brought with us, some *otak-otak* from Banten." (*Otak-otak* is a kind of delicacy made from fish paste which is wrapped in leaves and grilled on an open fire. It is really delicious with the proper sauces.) I found myself regretting I had not stayed around to receive the *otak-otak*. I said to Gus Dur, "Unfortunately, I am at home now. Too bad I did not get the *otak-otak*." And the president said, "It's okay, don't worry. I will save it for you in the refrigerator." I said, "Great, thank you. I will get it tomorrow morning." I thought that was really neat. It was a unique touch. In my mind's eye I could see the president placing the fish paste snacks in the refrigerator for me.

The next day during lunch after a cabinet meeting, I casually joked, "Oh, by the way, is my *otak-otak* still in the refrigerator?" He said, "Oh, yes," and he called his aide and said, "Bring *Pak* Wimar's *otak-otak* to him so he can take it home." I interjected, "Hmm ... better still, could you please give it to my driver, so he can put it in my car?"

So it was given to my driver and I continued working with the president until about 4 o'clock when official visiting hours ended. We then sat around talking about the day's events, which was full of the aftermath of the first memorandum and the reactions of the press. Contrary with what people might believe, the mood was upbeat, because we believed the president's innocence would carry him through the ridiculous corruption charges. This was not a corrupt man and we laughed at people who could even think that way. There were enough people who knew Gus Dur's simple lifestyle for us to be sure the false accusations would backfire later.

While President Wahid never took political issues lightly he would invariably conduct analysis in a relaxed atmosphere. Tactical discussions were as leisurely as philosophical discourses. Gus Dur just could not operate in a pedantic way. He liked to see the big picture in the same frame as the small details, switching back and forth effortlessly. His language was as informal as his thinking was disciplined. But he had too much respect for the individual to dictate how others should think or how thinking teams should be organized. As a result his personal analysis would be incisive but the inputs tend to be scattered. At best, we would have his sharp mind and his database work with a group of diverse backgrounds. His access to people was not dictated by compartments of rank or position. He could call anyone or even meet anyone whom he considered relevant to an issue. More often than not it would be people from the media or the civil society.

That was the situation on the day when Memorandum I fed the public appetite for political drama. In the eye of the storm, President Wahid was serene. The only time he got upset was when the Golkar said the president had committed a public lie. I was furious myself, but we kept our cool in public. In the president's office, a few of us had gathered to go over the day's events sipping cups of tea and coffee. We had invited one of our close friends from a major daily and the conversation went on in a rambling way, punctuated by phone calls and requests for more tea and snacks. We were cruising along until the president asked Yenny, who had joined us in this after-hours chat, to bring out some of the *otak-otak* for us to eat. She said, "They're all gone." He said, "What do you mean, *gone?*" "Well, you gave the last package away to *Pak* Wimar." He said, "What?!?" I said, "Oh, I'm sorry. No problem, I can get it from the car." He said, "No, no, those are yours to take home. But how come my supply is finished?" And Yenny said, "Well, we all ate it." This made Gus Dur frown. He seemed more upset by the missing delicacies than by any political news received that day. Fortunately the ever resourceful Yenny somehow came up with a serving of *otak-otak* which shifted the discussion back on track. As a matter of fact the talk was as good as the snacks. Later I asked Yenny where she got the *otak-otak*. She did not say, but I suspect they belonged to her mother.

The Three Tenors

Yahya, Adhie and I stumbled into the unprecedented position of spokesmen in October 2000. We were not opera singers but in my vanity I thought of ourselves as Domingo, Carreras and Pavarotti called in for a command performance. There were really four spokesmen, but one was appointed *ex officio*: the Chief of the Presidential Press Bureau, Dharmawan Ronodipuro, an excellent professional who was pulled in from the private sector just like the rest of us. The difference was that the three of us

Lunch with the president and the three spokesmen (Yahya Staquf and Adhie Massardi standing) and Cabinet Secretary Marsillam Simandjuntak as the daily regulars. The food in the presidential complex was the same for all 300-something people except for Gus Dur, who only ate string beans, fruit and other health foods.

were directly recruited by the president, and none of us really knew why. Maybe it was different for Yahya who was the most qualified choice. Not only was he deputy secretary general of PKB, the president's political party, but he was also a son of a great *kiai*, entitling him to be called *Gus* Yahya just like *Gus* Dur. These credentials are a guarantee of loyalty and an understanding of Gus Dur. Adhie is a talented writer who is quite prolific on various subjects. Like myself, he had never held a political position which would have made it easier to understand his elevation to a top political post. The three of us did not know each other and we reported for work separately.

I felt like one of the Three Bears visiting Goldilocks. Everything came in threes. Three desks, three telephone sets, three tailor-made suits. I was officially the Chief with the task of coordinating, but in my style I chose a collegial mode, each being pro-active and independent. I suggested we start in a reactive mode because a programmed mode would be at odds with the style of the president and media challenges which came from all directions. Besides, we had to operate with no resources except our wit and our words.

It must be interesting to look at the three of us, tenors by no means, performing in remarkably perfect synchronization throughout our brief career in government. Our results are probably negligible and our performance debatable, but we did find the synergy that made our time with the president very productive and so much to his liking that after we were dissolved along with the Wahid presidency, the three of us have remained very close associates of Gus Dur.

You're Fired!

One of the themes the public loved to pick on was the way positions and people were shuffled around so much. In the spin of the instant analyst, this was seen as a negative without regard to the reasons for the changes. Turnover was quite high in the government of Gus Dur. From October 1999 to February 2001, a total of three cabinet reshuffles took place. A further round of musical chairs marked the final weeks of the Wahid presidency. These reshuffles are often pointed out as a weakness of the Wahid presidency. I don't think the case is that clear-cut. First, many of the replacements were done in the cause of improvement. They were inspired either by poor performance of the incumbents or damaging lack of discipline within the government. When a football team keeps losing games, coaches often look at their material and try put different combinations of people to face certain situations. While no one can refute the incompetence of some members of the Wahid-Megawati government, whenever President Wahid made changes the very people who criticized the cabinet cried foul.

Let us take a few examples. Ryaas Rasyid, the person who is closely identified with regional autonomy, started his public career in the education institution for the civil service. In the public consciousness, his name was identified with regional autonomy and later on with decentralization when he picked up the issue in the final period of Soeharto's rule. Going into Habibie's government, Ryaas had become an authority, and when Gus Dur formed his first cabinet Ryaas Rasyid, being relatively untainted by the New Order, became the logical choice for Minister of State for Regional Autonomy. This was to deal with the ambitious plan of shifting power and bureaucratic focus from the central government to the level of *kabupaten*, or the sub-provincial level. This meant a huge amount of legal work, bureaucratic upheaval and employment shifts.

Ryaas Rasyid is a very hard working man. As the minister of state for regional autonomy he was very active:

President Wahid's presence brought all events down to human scale as I joked around with Minister Surjadi with Megawati listening with a smile.

speaking on television and radio, being quoted in
newspapers, attending seminars and officiating workshops
and appearing at parliamentary hearings.

In the second Wahid cabinet, which was inaugurated
in August 2000, Ryaas Rasyid was moved to the Ministry of
State for Administrative Reform. This is where the trouble
set in for Mr. Rasyid. He had actually anticipated a
promotion, because in the process of forming the new
cabinet he was appointed as one of the three team members
to propose the new structure of the cabinet along with Susilo
Bambang Yudhoyono and Erna Witoelar. Of course that
did not bring any real claim to job security. But a lot of people
thought that Ryaas Rasyid would be the logical choice for
promotion to the minister of home affairs, a position that
was held by retired General Surjadi Soedirdja.

When Ryaas Rasyid did not get the job for minister
of home affairs, he moved to the Ministry for Administrative Reform with great reluctance. His performance
in that new position did not match at all the energy and
the dedication that he had put into his job in the Ministry
for Regional Autonomy. Instead of accepting the new
challenge he maintained his role as the architect of regional
autonomy and still spoke out as the 'expert' on such issues,
in some circles being quite critical of the slow pace of
developments in implementing regional autonomy. In
cabinet meetings he often found himself in conflict with
other ministers on all kinds of issues. The arguments and
debates were quite open, but he did not contribute
positively to the synergy or to the working climate within
the cabinet. When his differences of opinion with other
ministers became untenable, the president stopped calling
on him to discuss matters of importance. This made Rasyid
even more impatient and he started speaking like a person

who had lost control. Credit should be given to Rasyid for never showing disloyalty to either the president or the vice president, but he often did disservice to himself by portraying himself as a person without a role. Form followed function when the president terminated his position, leaving his ministry vacant. Rasyid then went into active opposition in the public, bringing with him people like Andi Malaranggeng, a bright young political scientist. But when Rasyid became critical of Gus Dur, Andi Malaranggeng followed suit. Actually he had been considered to take the place of Rasyid or to take the lead in regional autonomy through a special body, but Malaranggeng chose instead to become a gadfly television personality.

One of the other controversial cases of termination from Gus Dur's cabinet was even more clear-cut. This was the case of Yusril Ihza Mahendra, the smooth talking lawyer who rose up in Soeharto's State Secretariat under Moerdiono, becoming a speechwriter of Soeharto. His professorship at his young age showed diligence in attending to his academic and administrative chores at the University of Indonesia. Yusril is also very ambitious and declared himself a presidential candidate in 1999 on the basis of his chairmanship of the Star and Crescent Party (PBB)—a party which gained about two percent in 1999 elections. His candidacy never materialized into anything except added leverage in the Central Axis headed by Amien Rais. He became a strong political figure with a shaky base. When he was offered the Ministry of Justice and Human Rights in Gus Dur's cabinet, he took it with enthusiasm. Throughout his work as cabinet minister, Yusril performed with a high degree of diligence although his professionalism often conflicted with his political goals.

Soon his talent as a legal expert was overshadowed by his politics and negative comments on Wahid's presidency. Quite often he would disagree with the president on matters of importance; for example the possibility of the decree banning the Assembly and how to deal with the arrest of Tommy Soeharto. Finally he became an opposition element within the cabinet which was not helpful.

As his communications with Gus Dur diminished, his closeness to Vice President Megawati increased. And in the days when he was debating what kind of role he would play, he would very often be seen to be dropping by the vice president for consultation. When Yusril began to announce in public that the president should step down, Gus Dur was left with no choice but to ask him to resign. Yusril had openly declared a difference of opinion with the president, claiming the president's policies were ill-advised and erroneous. Yusril then put on a public show of being unjustly fired, and resumed his politicking with Megawati. When Megawati picked her cabinet, Yusril was one of her easiest choices.

The other cases of dismissal from Gus Dur's cabinet also had to do with the problematic situations from the incumbent. Some also improved the team, such as replacing Marzuki Darusman with the courageous and incorruptible Baharuddin Lopa and later, after Lopa's untimely death, Gus Dur put in a public favorite for attorney general, Marsillam Simandjuntak.

In a situation of transition, in which cabinet performance was shaky at best, the decision not to stick with problematic people and to replace them with better ones, was in my view clearly a better choice. Perhaps the mistake was in the beginning to have settled for people with dubious loyalty and dubious capabilities. But changing a bad or inappropriate person with a better person is always a sound management decision. It was not seen the same way by most of the press. They preferred a cabinet which stays in place like in the Soeharto days. They stay for five years with no changes regardless of how the minister performed. Of course Soeharto exacted very tight control on his ministers, so nothing ever went dramatically astray—except, of course, the nation as a whole.

Cabinet Meetings

There were many political highs in our time with Gus Dur. Some came with formal political decisions and events but many happened away from the public eye. But the most tangible feeling of legitimacy usually came at the bi-weekly cabinet meetings. The ritual became very pleasant after a while because you had a sense of being the authority of the land and of the availability of the state apparatus that is designed to apply that authority. Cabinet meeting were usually held every other Thursday. On these days I would be geared up to work the full day at the palace. I would be sure to get a good night's rest the night before. On cabinet day I would leave home early—but not so early as to get midmorning drowsiness.

Cabinet meetings were scheduled to start at 9 o'clock. I would arrive at the palace at 8 o'clock, coming in from the back 'insiders' entrance—the steps leading to the foyer and banquet room. There you have two sets of formal seats. Usually people would be sitting around in informal and measured casualness. Of course there were the ubiquitous palace staffers, the security guards and people who seemed to be a bit of both. I would take my place on one of the chairs. Like in high school, people

The president was always surrounded by security— much less than his predecessor, but still secure. We were lucky to have excellent officers in the Presidential Security Force, with whom we have remained friends up until the present day.

tended to drift towards their favorite seats. I learned to position myself where I could keep an eye on all the doors leading into that central room.

One door was connected to the president's private quarters at the east wing of the building, and another one to the west wing where the presidential office is located. At 8:30 or 8:45 the president would come out from one of the two wings. He would be escorted by his adjutant, one or two security people, and his hand would be guided by his private assistant, Munib Huda.

He had four adjutants, one each from the different branches of the Armed Forces and the Police. Colonel Sabar Yudho was the first adjutant I came to know personally—even before I was approached to become the chief presidential spokesman—when I was moderator for the National Consultation Forum in Bali on 30 June 2000. The second adjutant I came to know was Navy Colonel

Room Effendi, who was always spic and span, and like all the adjutants, physically very fit. I had met him for the first time at the Jakarta Hilton Hotel when I was called in to meet Gus Dur. The third adjutant was Air Force Colonel Sukirno who seems to have come from the background of Gus Dur's traditional supporters, and then Police Colonel Sutarman. All struck me as very professional and genuine people.

One of these adjutants would escort Gus Dur out from wherever he was into the main hall which would lead to the exit in the back. I would join them in the middle of the room and announce my name. That's how you always start your day with Gus Dur. You have to announce your name since he cannot see you. I would say, "Wimar Witoelar, Gus" and he would say, "Oh, hi! Good morning!" and then shake my hand. Always gentle and upbeat. We would all walk out to the east side in the back. There two golf buggies would be waiting to take the president from the palace to the Bina Graha building. When I was lucky I would be invited to sit in next to Gus Dur in the golf cart. The vehicle has two seats each at the front and back. The front seats were occupied by the driver and the adjutant and the back seat was for the president and the lucky person that morning. If there was a breakfast guest of high rank or having urgent topics to discuss, he would sit next to Gus Dur. Often it would be Alwi Shihab or some other senior member of the cabinet. In that case I would sit in the second car.

The procession with the golf carts had to travel maybe four hundred meters from the palace to the Bina Graha building, taking a ninety-degree turn at the building at the rear, Istana Negara. Making a turn to the right took us parallel to Jalan Veteran. Approaching Bina

Graha my adrenaline would be pumped up. I could see clusters of reporters waiting with their notepads, mikes and television cameras. It was a positive anticipation because I like to deal with the press. When there were difficult issues I would make sure I had thought things out and prepared some decent answers.

Gus Dur is never perturbed by a crowd. That is actually a problem because he tends to respond to any question thrown out in any form by any reporter, and that's not always the prudent thing to do. Loose questions invite loose answers but only the answers get publicized. Gus Dur, being the open and free man that he is, never shies away from the press. That is something for which he should be given credit. He was treating the country to unprecedented open dialogue and making the presidency accessible for the reporters and the people.

We would wade through the reporters and step into the ground floor of Bina Graha building. This is a Soeharto-era building, a bit of socialist architecture with

Arriving at the Bina Graha presidential office after the doorstep Q&A which happened throughout the day.

lots of concrete and intimidating straight lines and glass panes. But it is functional, provides plenty of space and offers a very good cabinet room. Before we went into the cabinet room we would go into the presidential office to the left of the foyer, East side. There are actually two presidential offices on top of each other, one at the ground floor and one at the second floor. They are connected by a small elevator. We would pass the ground floor office, take the elevator and stop at the second floor office which connects through a small hallway into the cabinet room.

It is in this presidential office that we would wait and make small talk with whomever happened to be there. Usually there were three or four people including the president. Many important things were discussed here in these semi-private conversations, being as it was the first meeting of the day for many seeking Gus Dur's opinions. The purpose of lingering around was to wait for the vice president to arrive. She usually arrived quite punctually, five minutes before the 9 o'clock meeting. When she came in, polite handshakes were the norm. Megawati would smile courteously at each of us but she never went beyond that courtesy. The others would say, "How are you?", "How are you doing?", "Everything alright?" Without further ado then the president would say, "Let's go." So off we would go, taking the few steps into the cabinet room. Three or four people made up the typical procession, including the president and the vice president, flanked by the adjutant and security guards. Ministers and other participants of the meeting would already have assembled, entering through a separate door from the wide side of the room.

The meeting room is dominated by a doughnut-shaped conference table which seated about forty cabinet officers. There is a concentric outer ring for the noncabinet members. That's where I had my seat, at the back to the right of the president and the vice president. I would take my place and put on the headphone set. The person at my left would be Professor Djunaedi Hadisoemarto, chief of Bappenas, the National Planning Agency. These seats were like benches in school, everybody had their seats and people didn't move around from their assigned places (unless of course they got reshuffled). The meeting was usually opened by Gus Dur, very often with a small joke and an important statement. After that he would revert to Megawati, saying that he invited the vice president to chair the meeting while he listened in or sometimes stepped out to do other work.

Megawati would chair the meeting in an orderly fashion where each minister was given a turn to submit a report or announce plans. Marsillam, as cabinet secretary, did not think highly of these cabinet meetings since they were quite ritualistic. But I found them useful because they offered a chance to put everything on the table in a comprehensive manner and see how each minister would deliver his or her report.

The meeting usually ended on time, and if there was a delay, usually it was not more than thirty minutes in length. In fact some cynics said that Megawati's main skill is in making sure meetings run on time—not by necessarily organizing the substance of discussion, but by giving people specific time allocations to have their say. Some of these cabinet meetings were more interesting than others, as when there were important issues or when ministers expressed their feelings towards each other. The most memorable cabinet meeting was on 12 March as we were being circled by student demonstrators with Amien Rais lurking outside (but more on this later).

During the bi-weekly cabinet meetings, the president was usually flanked by Minister Susilo Bambang Yudhoyono and Megawati.

International Encounters

Foreign policy was President Wahid's forté and we had frequent discussions on the subject. We covered current and historical events and went over his policies. Streams of ambassadors came to the presidential office, both our own posted abroad and those representing other countries. The president relished these meetings and treated them as training modules in foreign affairs management. As foreign minister, Alwi Shihab was a close confidant of President Wahid. This was policy making on the go, and I have no idea how the Foreign Ministry kept up, but we had frequent briefings and debriefings with Alwi's staff. As we took so many foreign trips I met quite a lot of these Foreign Ministry-types. Many of them struck me as competent—even impressive—in foreign policy matters. I felt President Wahid was quite comfortable with the Foreign Ministry establishment, although he characteristically chafed at the rules dictated by protocol so loyally nurtured by the Ministry's protocol officers. Several foreign policy issues stood out in the ten months I was in the presidential office.

We had many meetings with heads of state and heads of government. I attended three which were held in Jakarta, respectively with Prime Minister Atal Behari Vajpayee of India, President Cardozo of Brazil and Prime Minister Kim Dae Jung of South Korea. Prime Minister Kim, who had spent thirty years as an opposition leader surviving assassination attempts and political oppression, cautioned Gus Dur that reform is always a dangerous job. Kim also went out of his way to warn Gus Dur against a hostile press and disloyal members of the government. In private conversation they seemed very close although none spoke the other's language and Kim spoke only faltering English. Still you could feel the kinship of lifelong defenders of democracy.

Korean PM Kim Dae Jung is antithetical in style to Gus Dur but they share mutual admiration as lifelong advocates of human rights and democracy.

President Wahid attended many multilateral gatherings in his brief period in office, from international Islamic conferences to APEC meetings to the United Nations General Assembly. He also picked up numerous honorary degrees from world-renowned universities. These were achievements I admired because they went beyond the standard accolades normally given to heads of state. And the orations he gave were classic expressions of public philosophy. Most noteworthy are those at the Sorbonne in Paris, Columbia University in New York and the practical thoughts outlined at the Asian Institute of Technology in Bangkok. These landmarks are even more awesome as they were all delivered without text and without reading preparation. I always had the conviction that in many ways Gus Dur was too big a man to be confined to national borders. In fact, in the year I was with him the international appreciation went far beyond the careless treatment he received from the Indonesian public. He was always suave and charming in cross-border interaction. One multilateral forum I attended in its entirety was the ASEAN Summit held in Singapore in February 2001.

The meeting concentrated on projects with direct economic interests to the countries in which the projects are located. The island archipelagic region of ASEAN was not touched in a direct way by these projects, and that was one topic the Indonesian delegation was instructed by the president to address. In a wider sense, ASEAN evolved—in President Wahid's eyes—from an association of solidarity among nations into a more pragmatic association relating to mutual economic interests, which was fine in principal. But there are still many issues of justice and social development in the territory which ASEAN encompasses.

For Indonesia the prime issue was East Timor. Could it be admitted to ASEAN in order to benefit from the economic support and protection it could have in this family of nations, or could it at least be addressed as a country for which ASEAN projects are designated? Before he raised the issue at the ASEAN meeting, President Wahid had a confidential meeting with Senior Minister Lee Kuan Yew of Singapore. I was not present at the meeting but the president talked to me immediately afterwards and he was not very happy with the way the discussion with SM Lee had gone. The rest is on public record that he had some harsh words for Singapore along the lines of what he told me on that morning, which was that Lee Kuan Yew thinks East Timor should not be welcomed into ASEAN because it would just, in SM Lee's view, be extra baggage for the ASEAN nations.

Gus Dur did not like that and he thought that if ASEAN could not be an association of solidarity then Indonesia would have to find its own ways to deal with these issues. So he came up with the idea of a West Pacific Forum that could include at least East Timor, Indonesia and Australia and eventually to be expanded to Papua New Guinea, then New Zealand and the Philippines. I thought that was an idea which made sense so I was glad when President Wahid outlined a diplomatic plan to socialize the idea and in fact instructed Rizal Ramli and I to look at some of the practical economic aspects of such a forum.

This idea was justified in Gus Dur's mind on the grounds that in today's community of nations, multilateral associations are no longer exclusive. In the case of ASEAN, many members of ASEAN already have concurrent multilateral agreements such as Singapore's military pact with New Zealand and Australia. Also, Malaysia and

Singapore Prime Minister Goh Chok Tong at the ASEAN summit, my multilateral debut. "I have seen you around," he said. He must watch a lot of television.

Indonesia had ties with the organization of Islamic nations. So several multilateral associations could coexist side by side, each catering to the specific province of interest. For ASEAN this notion had special significance because when it was founded in 1967 there was a romantic notion attached to it as it brought together nations which had never before held a dialogue. Indonesia had just come out from under Soekarno's isolationism and President Soeharto issued the first feelers to Malaysia to set up a regional grouping as an entity which gathered together the young nations politically—more or less on a platform of anti-Communism. That is why Vietnam and the socialist countries were not included in the first ASEAN. Now of course the situation has changed and the necessity for such an organization has also become outdated.

President Wahid's position was to work with ASEAN where it was still useful but to be watchful if it

tried to re-orient itself. In his view, if the majority of
ASEAN wished it to be merely a development project
organization then so be it, even if it turned out to be more
to the benefit of the mainland countries. But Indonesia's
future would be invested in an association with specific
missions based on the West Pacific Forum concept. This
idea beyond the ASEAN summit was one the president
discussed among diplomats and foreign ministry officials
of Indonesia and some associates in Australia and the
Philippines. Were it not for the sudden termination of Gus
Dur's presidency, there could have been some interesting
developments in the West Pacific Forum.

Indonesia's stance in the ASEAN Summit was not to place
undue emphasis on the technical deliberations. The
delegation was to exercise due diligence and take care of
Indonesia's position as part of the community of the
ASEAN nations. The bilateral meetings held during the
summit were considered to be much more important. I
was involved in several of these. One memorable event
was the official bilateral meeting with the Chinese
delegation led by Prime Minister Zu Rongji. It was very
finely orchestrated and very formal. The delegations faced
each other in rows of about twenty people each in one of
the staterooms of the Shangri-La Hotel and just sat stony-
faced as President Wahid and Prime Minister Zu sat in
front exchanging remarks.

I was quite proud to see that while Zu used an
interpreter, my president did not. As usual, Gus Dur was
quite open and candid while presenting some very
important concepts of cooperation between China and
Indonesia. Among others this covered a railroad in
Kalimantan and Chinese participation in the development

of high technology, specifically computer applications. Of course as always Gus Dur spoke from memory and his own basic intelligence. He never uses notes since he cannot read them. The bilateral summit meeting was brief but productive. Several cooperative economic ventures were highlighted and expressed in protocols of cooperation.

A bilateral meeting of a different kind was held with Prime Minister Mahathir Mohamad of Malaysia, which came in the form of a breakfast meeting. Dr. Mahathir and his ministers came to President Wahid's suite at 7 o'clock and stayed for one hour. It was a small meeting, just four from the Malaysian side and four from the Indonesian side including myself. What impressed me about this meeting was that it really was informal. Mahathir has a style which is very unique. Possessing immense charisma, he is an assertive person and obviously erudite and intelligent, but also quite experienced and harsh. It sent chills up my spine to hear affairs of state being addressed in such a personal and confident manner. It was as if the world did not matter outside of these two

A very formal China-Indonesia bilateral meeting during the ASEAN Summit in Singapore. President Wahid was speaking without an interpreter.

leaders. This was one meeting where Gus Dur's profile
was mild compared to Mahathir's belligerent style. If Gus
Dur was described later in the week as being very hard on
Singapore, you would not have gained that impression in
this informal meeting. Here Gus Dur was the mild one
and Mahathir gave some sharp and candid observations
about relations with Singapore.

In public, President Wahid came out as very harsh
when he pointed some features of Singaporean political
behavior which was detrimental to relations between our
two countries. The honesty in which Gus Dur conducted
his public dialogue damaged his public relations in the
end. The media preys on non-standard quotes, and
certainly he never spoke in public relations clichés. My
dilemma was to choose between continuing to display his
genuine thoughts or burying them behind a façade of
public relations cosmetics. I may be at fault for not limiting
President Wahid's press exposure, but I felt his place in
history was not to continue the past but to stimulate fresh
beginnings. So while Senior Minister Lee Kuan Yew did
not attract any comment for his reluctance to promote
ASEAN support for the weak fledgling state of East
Timor, it was President Wahid who bore the brunt of
public displeasure by revealing his commitment to help
our brothers in the east. It reflected the constant irony of
style over substance.

The ASEAN Summit was very efficiently organized by the Singapore event organizers—all credit goes to
them. I do not think that the death knoll of ASEAN has
sounded, but it has changed character completely since
1967. The summit meeting this time seemed almost like a
corporate board meeting—and being held in Singapore
made the impression all the stronger.

Bulogate and Bruneigate

In the end, it was not at all clear on what 'issues' Gus Dur fell from power. There was never any doubt in my mind that he was innocent of the charges leveled against him in the context of the Bulogate and Bruneigate scandals. Yet by the time parliamentary leaders and the press were done with their massive public opinion campaign the public had come to associate these two scandals with President Wahid. They made charges without proof that Gus Dur had been involved in these two cases of misuse of public funds.

Bruneigate refers to the case in which the Sultan of Brunei contributed US$2 million for the cause of Aceh. According to the allegations, Gus Dur used these funds for personal or political purposes. Bulogate was a more complicated case. According to one version, Gus Dur had received money from the pension funds of Bulog, the state logistics agency, in the equivalent of US$4 million. Again, it was alleged that these funds were used for Wahid's private and political purposes.

One of the first questions I put to Gus Dur on our very first walk around the palace in the wee hours of that October morning in 2000 was whether he had received money from the Bulog pension fund or whether he even knew about it. Gus Dur said, "No, of course it's not true. I know nothing about the money." I persisted with questions about Suwondo, the masseur who was supposed to have been the go-between in getting money out of the Bulog pension funds, the Yanatera Foundation, into Gus Dur's hands. At that time Suwondo had been just apprehended in a bungalow south of Jakarta, somewhere up in the mountains approaching Puncak. I asked if the president knew that Suwondo had been arrested, and whether he actually worked for the president in securing the illegal money. Gus Dur said he knew that Suwondo had been arrested, but he knew nothing about his actions. Whatever he did, Suwondo must have been doing it for himself or whoever his friends happened to be.

I was basically satisfied with his answer, because I had to start out with the premise that the president of this country was enlisting me to his cause in sincerity and honesty. So in this instance I let the matter go, but I picked it up again at random whenever I heard the case being discussed either by the president or by others. On all occasions I was satisfied with the answers that asserted Gus Dur's innocence. But the questions refused to go away because they were driven by a definite political agenda, which was to distract Gus Dur from finding his form and get on with the business of reform.

The cases are too complicated to go into here. But the charges against Gus Dur were never proven, either by Parliament's special committee on Bulogate and Bruneigate, or by the Attorney General's office. The press and public opinion, and certainly his political opposition, gave a much stronger verdict than the law or any court of logic.

The Bruneigate and Bulogate scandals proved to be the start of the undoing of President Wahid's presidency. This was not part of my original expectation. I thought since the president was innocent, he would eventually emerge victorious from these accusations and turn the table around against his accusers. I was to learn the harsh lesson that in post-Soeharto Indonesia, politics does not work like that. When the accusers failed to provide the case with convincing evidence of Gus Dur's wrongdoing, they just simply moved to a different accusation.

Bruneigate and Bulogate remain unsolved cases and, to the disappointment of Gus Dur's supporters, were never

With the domestic and international press in the reception room used for large press conferences. The frequency and intensity of media contact was unprecedented.

really aired in complete form. There was the 'white book' by PKB, Gus Dur's party base, which came out with the full story of Bruneigate and Bulogate. But it came too late, when public opinion had already confirmed its suspicion of something being wrong with Wahid's handling of the money. I suppose you cannot blame the public because in the Soeharto period you could constantly hear official statements which had no credibility whatsoever. In the case of Bruneigate, the denials and the explanation actually came forth in an official address to Parliament by then-Justice Minister Baharuddin Lopa, in response to the first parliament memorandum. It was an excellent and clear exposition. Yet it met with no positive response, so successful was the public opinion cabal of the press against Gus Dur.

To this day, Bruneigate and Bulogate remain big question marks, but as far as I am concerned Gus Dur was at worst guilty only of messy handling of a messy case. Gus Dur certainly underestimated the power of the press in turning speculation into conviction. I overestimated the good sense of the public.

The President and the Fugitive

After Gus Dur was removed from the presidency, Bruneigate and Bulogate ceased to capture the public imagination. In fact Bulogate soon came to refer to the second scandal in which Akbar Tandjung, the chairman of Parliament, was indicted for funneling Bulog money for his private purposes. But when Tommy Soeharto was finally captured in December 2000 the police leaked some testimony made by him and his lawyer that accused Gus Dur of extortion in exchange for some favors in lightening Tommy's prison burden. The press coverage focused not so much on what his crimes actually were and what it meant for the nation to have him arrested, but whether Gus Dur had something to do with Tommy's going into hiding.

According to some theories, Tommy became a fugitive because he was disappointed when President Wahid failed to give him a pardon or commutation of his sentence. There was no discussion as to who actually stage-managed Tommy's year of hiding from the law—although that would provide priceless information on crimes committed in harboring a known fugitive, and also would expose the corrupt nature of some elements of the police and other state apparatus.

Instead, the press focused on a meeting Tommy had one day in October 2000 with then President Wahid. In the popular press, that meeting was suspected to have resulted in some kind of deal between Tommy and the president: either to provide sanctuary for Tommy or to release him from prosecutions by a pardon or cancellation of the charges against him. No matter that such a deal never transpired, no matter that there was no evidence at all of President Wahid having received any favors from

Tommy or anyone else, the public still loved notions of an underhanded deal going on between a glamorous convict and a president easily harassed in the press.

The meeting with Tommy actually happened before I was fully brought into the loop on the president's activities. I only learned about the meeting after it had happened. President Wahid said he had met Tommy Soeharto upon Tommy's request at the Hotel Borobudur. I wondered aloud why the president would do such a thing. He said he did not see anything wrong in seeing anyone especially if they requested to see you. At that time Tommy had been recently convicted of a real estate scam—though not yet a fugitive—and Gus Dur was interested to hear what he had to say. It is a matter of public record now that the meeting in Hotel Borobudur and a subsequent meeting at the Hotel Regent did not produce any agreements. President Wahid let the judicial process continue and eventually Tommy's request for a review of his case was

The media have defined my public role over the last eight years, and we tried hard to use the preciously new concept of a free press without going over the edge.

rejected by the court and Tommy was ordered into custody. That was the part in which I got involved. After meeting with Attorney General Marzuki Darusman and Justice Minister Yusril Ihza Mahendra, Tommy was ordered to be detained. Tommy went into hiding and was allowed to run free in a pitiful game of hide-and-seek for more than a year before his capture on the last day on duty of Police Chief Bimantoro.

Throughout my days with President Wahid we constantly asked for reports on Tommy's whereabouts from the Attorney General's office and from the National Police. But the president was as helpless as the public in receiving reports and promises from the police that Tommy was just a few days away from capture. This hurt President Wahid's credibility as the public found it hard to believe that the president knew nothing of Tommy's whereabouts.

So the president was kept in the dark on Tommy. We felt somebody must know where he was, as it would be impossible for a person to hide for so long without the protection of some people in power and the collaboration of some people in the police. As for the meeting in the hotel, that was the last contact between the president and Tommy, and no deal was made. When Tommy won his court review it was long after Gus Dur ceased to be president and only after the murder of the judge who had convicted him. Even now I don't understand why the police insisted on pursuing the topic of the meetings between Gus Dur and Tommy. As Tommy himself explicitly denied making payments to Gus Dur and it was proven that no deal was made, Gus Dur's contacts with Tommy before he became a fugitive hardly mattered except to a sensationalist press.

Showdown at the Convention Center

Going back to the period of President Wahid's persecution by the political elite, the feeling was that of a disease slowly creeping in though we thought it would not be a problem because our body was in good health. The main problem with the constant haranguing of the politicians in Parliament was that it became very difficult for the government to do anything, let alone pick up momentum on reform. I felt it was ironic how the media played up the public harassment of the government while covering very little of the efforts made by the president and some of his ministers to meet public expectations. The contacts the president made with peace-seeking people in Aceh and Maluku, support for human rights trials related to East Timor, pressures on the attorney general to speed up prosecution of corruption cases, even President Wahid's urging of constitutional reform were very scantily covered in the press. The president made an excellent speech in Bandung on the anniversary of the association of judges, where he articulated the gaps in the constitution which allowed different interpretations of the division of rights and responsibilities between the president and Parliament. Although the media were present at the speech and I repeated the content of the speech in a press conference afterwards, they preferred instead to focus on the president's statement about Ajinomoto, a food additive.

Instead of going into a religious exposition on why it was all right for good Muslims to eat this certain brand of monosodium glutamate, he had university scientists explain its manufacturing process and showed the public that forbidden substances were not part of the product but rather passive catalysts which did not react with the goods in process. More significantly, he saw no problem with the disparity between his findings and those expressed by the MUI, a religious council which has long held the monopoly in religious opinion, but showing the disturbing habit of being instrumental in the disbursement of state power. In hindsight, President Wahid showed great courage in the food additive case by declaring that no single institution has the sole authority to represent principles and legalities in the application of Islamic customs and laws. But my point here is that while it is indeed an important subject, it was hardly in the same order of importance with the president's interpretation of the constitution and how resolution of its ambiguities might avoid a breakdown of constitutional practice.

Because of the ambiguity of the presidential/parliamentary relationship, the newly empowered parliament members had become overzealous in using their political power. Instead of being a legislative assembly with a mandate for government oversight, Parliament became judge, jury and executioner targeted solely on the president. At the height of Parliament activities against the president it was revealed that 150 pieces of legislation were overdue for finalization by Parliament. This included important legislation on regional autonomy, human rights courts and commercial law. The 500-member Parliament had only one thing on their agenda, and that was the investigation of the Bulogate and Bruneigate scandals. The specific process was being carried out by the 'Pansus', an acronym for the special committee formed to investigate the allegations. The Pansus were doing things normally done by an investigative body. In fact, they were roughly duplicating the Attorney General's office activities in looking at the

*With Cabinet Secretary Marsillam occasionally making announcements,
the give-and-take at our daily press briefings was sometimes sharp but
always friendly. Too bad the headlines often came out differently.*

corruption allegations. This made it awkward for the
president to cooperate. Although Gus Dur is always
ready to provide information, he felt he could not
compromise the authority of the presidential office in
allowing it to be summoned or interrogated at will by
the Pansus whose legal authority was unclear.

The media penchant for attacking the president
made every resistance to erosion of presidential authority
seem like a personal act of stubbornness on his part. There
was endless to and fro on whether the president could
properly be summoned by the Pansus and/or by Parliament, whether the Pansus should come to the president
or the other way around, evoking tiresome debate in press
articles, TV talk shows and seminars. This created a forum
for new parliamentarians to become television personalities, and it was frightening how personalities grew
increasingly more bizarre as the public spotlight rewarded
those who fed the media frenzy with sharp soundbites
against a vulnerable president.

At the urging of his legal advisers the president took
the initiative to meet with the Pansus. It was to be on neutral
ground, neither in the parliament nor in the presidential
office. The Jakarta Convention Center was chosen, and the
date was 22 January 2001. I came with the president in the

motorcade and we were met at the doorstep of the huge building by Bachtiar Chamsah, the committee chairman, Akbar Tandjung and various other politicians. After perfunctory greetings the group walked through the building and up the escalator to a meeting hall on the second floor. The members of the Pansus were already seated in the hall as the president and his staff took their places at the head of the rectangular placed table formation. The president was flanked by Luhut Pangaribuan, his legal adviser, Marsillam Simandjuntak, the Cabinet Secretary, Harun Al Rasyid, the constitutional expert, and other presidential aides. I sat behind the president waiting with anticipation for the fireworks to come.

Fireworks they were, although it was a case of very short blasts instead of a colorful display. The meeting which the press had billed as a showdown was an anticlimax. After a lengthy explanation by President Wahid on the chronology and facts of the Bulogate and Brunei cases he gave the floor to the parliamentarians. I breathed a sigh of relief because I thought the account was comprehensive and factual, shedding light on possibility of misrepresentations and misperception in both cases and leaving the investigation of criminality to the investigative and judicial processes. Then things went sour as parliamentarians spoke out with great energy asking for attention from each other and from the forum. As the chairman tried to present the questions in order the president asked what this forum was designed to be. Was it a consultation, a meeting for clarification, or an investigation? Because if it *was* an investigation, the president had no right to pervert his office by consenting to be interrogated by a body not equipped with the appropriate constitutional mandate.

Parliament is a constitutional partner of the president in the Indonesian Constitution, not a superior. And the Pansus as a parliamentary committee has no special investigative rights. Simple acquiescence to questioning would have been an irresponsible act of the president who is charged with upholding the constitution and the integrity of his office. The substance and the style of the President's response struck a sensitive nerve among the parliamentarians as they went off on an emotional binge. Standing and shouting for attention, they did not address the question of legality of the forum and instead insisted the president answer their questions on substance. On his part, the president declined to discuss substance until the specification of the forum was made clear. The politicians and the president chose not to connect. President Wahid ultimately declared he could not continue, stood up and left the hall. We all followed him out as Akbar Tandjung came up to us and asked what happened. He had been waiting outside and I just smiled at him. I knew at that moment that political developments would go downhill from then on.

❧

The Crisis of 12 March 2001

If John F. Kennedy had his moment of glory during the Cuban Missile Crisis of 1962, Gus Dur had his show of strength on 12 March 2001. I would describe the events on that day as an attempted grab for power using well organized student demonstrations. It started in February and came to an anticlimax on that day in March. Ever since 1966, March had been the month in which major political demonstrations seemed fated to occur. Soeharto's takeover

Police Col. Sutarman was one of four aides attached to the President, with Abdul Mujib Manan holding the key position of Presidential Secretary.

happened on 11 March 1966. The Malari anti-Japanese demonstrations and street burnings took place on 15 January 1974 with the aftermath stretching into detentions and political changes well into March. The student uprising against Soeharto (during which I was detained for a month as a faculty member at ITB) was scheduled in anticipation of the Assembly session in March 1978.

Trouble had been brewing since February 2001 with an increase of tension in the media and in public dialogue, pressing against the president. The issues varied according to occasion. Generally it revolved around charges of corruption in Bulogate, liberally interlaced with other perceived shortcomings of the Wahid presidency. The theme was that President Wahid was not competent, not capable of managing the government. These are valid judgments against any president, yet Gus Dur was a soft target because of the ease with which arbitrary attacks could incite a disillusioned public. It did not matter that the public discontent was fed by constant disruptions caused by covert elements who sought to destabilize the nation. Constant inflation, demonstrations, acrimony, bombings, all served to turn the public away from a government who were struggling to overcome the crisis.

Never before in Indonesian political history were students mobilized with such intense deployment of facilities and funds. The vehicle chosen for this campaign was the BEM (Badan Eksekutif Mahasiswa), an institution developed in many universities to engage the campus as a unit of political mobilization.

Driving in from the major cities and flying in from outside Java, student activists had meetings in Jakarta, unthinkable under normal circumstances when students have hardly enough resources even to travel from city to city. Anecdotal evidence points to certain individuals supporting these activities with generous amounts of capital. They have become household names in the folklore of political funding.

The student action fitted in very nicely with the diligence of the Pansus in Parliament, organized by the 'Senayan Cowboys'—parliamentarians against Gus Dur—who tried to use the Bulogate and Bruneigate rumors to implicate and impeach the president. The coordination was so smooth that often student demonstrators would march up to the parliament building and receive words of encouragement from the Pansus ringleaders like Bachtiar Chamsah (now cabinet minister under Megawati), Arifin Panigoro (the former Golkar politician and business partner of Soeharto arch-crony Ginanjar Kartasasmita turned chief fundraiser for Megawati) and lesser figures like PAN's Alvin Lie and PDI-P's Julius Usman.

The non-issues being bandied around by the anti-Wahid cabal saw passionate emotion compensating for lack of reason in the effort to push President Wahid out of office. The parallel between the Pansus and the BEM was such that on many occasions students consulted with the leader of Pansus and people like Bachtiar Chamsah, the chairman of Bulogate Pansus, who went so far as to welcome the students into the Parliament Building to support the Pansus. In they came, showing great camaraderie with their heroes in the Pansus. Amien Rais, the Chairman of the Assembly who had adopted the mission to unseat President Wahid as a personal vendetta, constantly gave moral support to the students and the Pansus whilst being apparently oblivious to his responsibilities as the chairman of the nation's supreme legislative council. Late February and March saw a constant stream of student demonstrations by BEM at the Parliament Building and the Hotel Indonesia roundabout and the main thoroughfares of Jalan Sudirman and Jalan Thamrin and finally at the Presidential Palace.

The anti-Gus Dur forces hit paydirt when the big day came and masses of people turned out. Falling well shy of their announced target of a general strike and promises to amass fifty thousand protesters, the demonstrations still managed to stop the city. Was that day, 11 March, the day on which Gus Dur would step down like his predecessor Soekarno? In the days leading up to 11 March, many public speakers and anti-Wahid student activists were already demanding that he resign from office and hand over the presidency to Vice President Megawati.

At that time, there were few signs of a fatal schism between Gus Dur and Megawati. Megawati did not openly endorse the student movement although she did not defend President Wahid either. Her party members in Parliament like Arifin Panigoro, Zulfan Lindan, Julius

Usman, Pramono Anung, Didi Supriyadi were strongly against Gus Dur, but Megawati herself and her husband Taufik Kiemas did not show signs of open disloyalty towards the president. This feature of the PDI-P political culture has always been puzzling to me, especially the apparent acceptance of this fuzzy positioning by Megawati.

The eleventh of March happened to be quiet, as it was a Sunday. The demonstrations did not really happen until Monday 12 March, when students began to accumulate in the city. It was also the date for a previously scheduled cabinet meeting. As the students started to gather on the street, we started to prepare for the cabinet meeting in the palace. The meeting dealt with routine issues of government while some of us followed developments outside through reports from friends over mobile phones. In my case I used a tiny digital radio pre-set for stations that specialized in reporting on demonstrations. Every thirty minutes Coordinating Minister of Politics, Security and Social Affairs Susilo Bambang Yudhoyono would give a brief roundup of what was happening outside. And although the crowd was building up, nobody in the room appeared flustered.

Megawati remained calm as usual, but then she must have known she was not personally threatened. In the case of Gus Dur, he was so used to students and mass movements that a crowd of fifty thousand in a metropolis of fifteen million was not worrisome. The pre-meeting talk with me that morning was not full of alarm. Gus Dur had simply speculated as to whether they would really be able to get together that number of people, and whether the pro-Gus Dur demonstrators would clash with them. He had asked his supporters not to be engaged in street conflicts, but we were always wondering how many would spontaneously show their support on the streets anyway because of the constant irritation by the manipulative media and outspoken politicians.

From various sources I learned that there was a special scenario organized for that day. The talk going around the streets was that Assembly Speaker Amien Rais himself would appear at the palace with the demonstrators, and would actually come up to the president and ask him to resign. That would be quite strange and outside all proper conventions of protocol, but it could be expected from a person like Amien. He has explained on numerous occasions that his position as Assembly Speaker did not diminish his right and obligation to act as party chairman or as a private citizen. This is just one example of the kinds of ethical issues that we had to grapple with, as many blur the line between personal interest and public mandate.

As that scenario, if it took place, would not threaten the constitutional and legal position of the president we did not worry about it too much. We also knew that the population at large did not share the feeling of animosity against Gus Dur. This seems to be very difficult for outside observers to understand, especially the international media. It is counter-intuitive for them to imagine that there are political sources of power outside the student movement, the press and the Parliament. But it is a fact in Indonesia and it was particularly relevant then because the student movement did not arise out of spontaneous grassroots anger as it did in the anti-Soeharto, anti-Habibie, or even anti-Soekarno demonstrations. Instead the student leaders were aspiring political activists who were organized at a very early stage in their student careers by experienced political operators.

The attitude of the media is a complicated matter.

Some journalists were undoubtedly paid to support the forces against Gus Dur, but I cannot believe that they represented a majority. Then there was the media's tendency to highlight controversy and exploit public impatience at the slowness of reform by the Wahid government, often succumbing to pure sensationalism. The belligerence of Parliament and the Pansus was a clear case of parliamentarians using their new freedom to flex political muscle and extract immediate personal gain. Money flowed like water to parliamentarians and reporters who were willing to play the game.

There is plenty of evidence of parliament members becoming immensely wealthy during the campaign against Gus Dur. Parliament members who spearheaded the anti-Wahid movement had become big spenders with conspicuous *nouveau riche* lifestyles: overnight, former Kijang owners began to drive around in ridiculously luxurious cars like Jaguars and Mercedes. Some suddenly owned multiple grand houses around town or even in Perth. These very same persons just two years before went around riding buses and did not have any assets to speak off. Again, formal evidence is difficult to gather as money laundering is the first skill acquired by bad politicians, and the courts were stacked against reform. Later on, Gus Dur's new attorney general, Baharuddin Lopa, tried to revamp the system, but that's another story.

It is very easy to see that the press, the students and Parliament did not represent the people because the general population did not rise up to support them as they did in the campaign against Soeharto and Soekarno. Ordinary people just looked on as the students with their color-coded university jackets marched yelling slogans prepared for them by their 'mentors'.

By 11 o'clock, things had become quite busy outside the palace. Inside, things remained calm. The cabinet room inside the Bina Graha building is sheltered from the outside world and the only windows were in the front foyer. So if you did not listen to the radio, or hear reports, life would seem to be very quiet and tranquil.

But we kept our alertness at peak level. Occasionally I would stroll out of the cabinet room and look outside through the window in the upstairs foyer. Lines of students seemed to be piled up in great numbers outside the palace. But news reports describe the crowd to be ten thousand in size at the palace, twenty thousand over all Jakarta. Again ten thousand is not a large number as mass demonstrations go, but with all the shouting and screaming outside the presidential compound, it did look to be a great number indeed.

Students were allowed by the palace guard to actually approach the presidential compound. They were leaning on the fence surrounding the compound, poking their hands through and even trading remarks with the security guards inside. This was against regulations for the Presidential Palace or as far as I know for seats of government elsewhere in the world at the presidential level. I don't think they would allow demonstrators to hang on the iron gates and fences of the White House in Washington DC, or at the Office of the Prime Minister in Canberra, or at Malacanang Palace in Manila. But here in Jakarta, on 12 March, students were shouting and banging the fences in front of the presidential security guards, and they felt quite safe.

When Minister Susilo Bambang Yudhoyono briefed us just before lunch, he was asked about the rumor that Amien Rais would come into the palace. Yudhoyono was asked how this would be dealt with if it happened. The established rule and the general consensus was that if *anybody* walked into the palace compound unannounced then he or she would be stopped. In fact he or she could be detained, even arrested. If the person resisted arrest, the notion became quite chilling. What can you do? You cannot shoot Amien Rais. But what if he insisted on entering, leading the students like a political pied piper?

In hindsight I saw that Megawati at that point showed exemplary loyalty to the president. During the whole day of 12 March, she did not once consult her private sources for activities outside. Nobody slipped notes to her or whispered reports, nor she did not ask anyone what was going on. She followed events like everyone else, through the public briefings in the cabinet room by Susilo Bambang and occasionally by the head of intelligence, General Arie Kumaat. And she was voicing opinions which clearly deplored the demonstrations and even disdain for the notion that Amien would show up at the demonstration.

We had our lunch break before the situation was resolved. By that time more students had accumulated. We heard that Amien did show up outside the Presidential Palace, which everybody inside and outside the palace saw on their television screens. I wondered at the time why the media never picked up this flagrant violation of ethics. The chairman of the nation's supreme legislative body, his wife, and members of parliament arrived by bus in the middle of the demonstration, parking the bus outside the palace. Amien actually addressed the students through a loud speaker, praising their militancy and endorsing their movement. Still the media dutifully pointed to Gus Dur— the legitimate president doing his job—as the source of the problem and not the victim.

It speaks volumes about the lack of ethics inside Parliament and the Assembly that the behavior of the Assembly's Chairman was not censured or even discussed. A Speaker of the Assembly had joined a student demonstration asking the legitimate president to step down in midterm. It boggled my mind to think about it. It is even more disappointing to see the 'responsible press' failing to pick up this significant abuse of power, blinded by their single-mindedness to follow the mob in the charge against the president.

From our side, in an interesting example of the openness of the Wahid presidency, we invited the leaders of the student demonstrators to appear at the press conference held daily by the presidential spokesmen. They failed to gain credibility when they doggedly clung to their demand for the president to step down without presenting clear reasons. In fact, in their list of demands they listed as number one the demand that President Wahid step down, and in number three they demanded that the president fix the economy. How can you fix anything if you step down? Having a son at the Institute of Technology at Bandung and having been Chairman of the ITB Student Council, I was ashamed that the current ITB student leaders could not present their case with any coherence.

In the end nothing happened because the student crowd did not build up to significant levels, nobody lost their temper inside the palace and Amien Rais backed away from his belligerent position against the president. Up until today people are wondering why he showed up at all at the demonstration, or whether he had a change in his plans. So he returned to the Assembly Building, the students dispersed and we went home. In the heat of the action, Megawati was offered safe passage to leave the palace by helicopter to avoid the crowd. To her credit, she declined. She said she would stay with us and leave the palace when the time was appropriate. So 12 March came and went, another tumultuous and strange episode in the colorful tenure of the Wahid presidency.

Ride to Bogor

Although the storming of the palace was shaken off, the trouble did not stop there. The opposition changed tactics and placed more emphasis on the press, feeding them bits of political fodder from the controlled Parliament. We fended for ourselves by working tirelessly with the press appealing to their good conscience. But it did not always work. Many good reporters still produced unprofessional articles. So we decided to try to offer the press an honest dialogue on a comprehensive set of issues. The date was set for Saturday to conduct a dialogue with the press in an open fashion. We wanted to try to eliminate all barriers of communication between the president and the press. And to do that, we decided for a change, we would like to have the meeting on an off-the-record basis. To provide a friendly and different climate, the president decided to hold the event at Bogor Palace, some fifty kilometers south of Jakarta.

I joined the president at the palace at 9 o'clock to leave for Bogor. The palace staff met me upon arrival and suggested I find Yenny, the president's daughter, immediately. I found Yenny quite concerned and anxiously waiting for me. She said the president was upset because of the developments over the first memorandum, which came out some days before. She was worried that Gus Dur might not be at his best for the press, unless he relaxed. So they had arranged for me to ride with the president in his official limousine. Yenny thought we could use the ride from the Presidential Palace to the Bogor Palace to cool things down a bit and get a more relaxed perspective.

Yenny then invited me to her computer room and we waited together for a printout from a website containing political jokes. She gave them to me and said maybe I could read them to her dad because he always enjoyed that sort of thing. I picked up the printout but never got to use it. As so often happens I found the president in a somewhat detached mood—not really intense, not really relaxed—but just removed from the things which were swirling on around him. It seemed to be his way of handling stress.

And when we got into the car and the motorcade left the palace, he started a conversation about Islamic music. He explained to me the difference between Arabic music and Islamic music. He is, of course, intimately familiar with both of them, and in fact sang me a few lines from each type of music. Later on he asked his adjutant to play a cassette of Islamic music, played by a prominent singer from the Middle East. So I aborted the plan to discuss political jokes and discussed music instead which engrossed the two of us practically for the full duration of the car ride to Bogor.

The president and I were very often involved in discussions on music and culture. However, I often had the feeling that as we talked, the other part of his mind was still on the political issues. And on this car ride to Bogor, we did occasionally switch to the issues of the day. I brought up the topic of the press conference and how we would handle it, and he brought up the topic of the opposition forces and how he would deal with their next move.

The president made use of the elegant Bogor Palace with its hectares of deer parks for an extensive and open luncheon talk—which some reporters later dismissed as non-productive.

Bogor turned out to be quite pleasant. For me it was the first visit to that palace, and it was almost as much a novelty as the visit to the Presidential Palace in Jakarta. Bogor Palace was impressive, serene, beautiful, with wide grounds and deer grazing around. In fact because there were so many deer and they kept multiplying, that the president at one point asked me to investigate the possibility of relocating some of those deer to a natural preserve in South Kalimantan. I talked to the Air Force Chief of Staff about this, but it turned out that the Hercules cargo aircraft could only transport twenty-five deer at one time, and the airlift would not be worthwhile if it did not move at least three hundred deer. So the plan was shelved, for a while at least.

The deer were there, waiting for us as we drove into the palace. The cool Bogor air in the midmorning was quite pleasant as reporters filed in. As always reporters are a source of liveliness, and Gus Dur and I enjoyed meeting with them and exchanged friendly remarks before we moved on to lunch.

The buffet had been prepared in the main halls of the palace. Besides the usual lunch buffet, we also had the specialty of the house, venison steak. Some venison was also presented in the form of *saté*, deer meat on skewers and roasted over an open fire—the delicious by-product of unavoidable culls.

Towards the end of the feast I stood up and walked to the rostrum with a mike. I welcomed the guests and the reporters, explained the ground rules emphasizing that the talks would be open. Everything would be answered in turn for the domestic and international press. But to make the session relaxed and productive, I asked the press to agree that the session would be on an off-the-record background basis. We didn't get any surprising questions. With the president whether it is off-the-record or on-the-record, the level of honesty remained the same, so it was pleasant but not quite eventful, although it helped in breaking the ice and getting the relationship between the palace press corps and the president and staff on a friendlier basis. I had always been friendly with the reporters and enjoyed the chance to simply chat. Some of them I had known for a long time preceding my duties in the presidential office.

The only blemish to the nice day came after we had adjourned. I watched television news at home, which featured an interview with Bambang Harymurti, chief editor of *Tempo* magazine, where he made some skeptical remarks about president's unwillingness to go on-the-record during the session in Bogor. I thought that was rather unfair, because the agreement to go off-the-record was reached with mutual consent, and in fact that enabled the discussion to be very free. And from our point of view, those comments were a manipulation of information on that session. This showed that the dark cloud had been gathering for a long time over the climate of communication that we wanted to build between the press and ourselves. No matter how hard we tried, some parts of the press were still more geared to emphasizing their skepticism and independence, rather than working together to listen to the message behind the noise.

Keeping to Non-Violence

Gus Dur is an ardent admirer of Mahatma Gandhi and his principle of non-violence. He has taken early initiatives to have the military quit its habit of violating human rights. It shows great ignorance when people fall for the propaganda that tried to paint him as condoning violence. The media made a lot of fuss in March 2001, when voices raised fear that fanatic supporters of Gus Dur would come to Jakarta from East Java and create public disturbances. This followed the demonstrations against Gus Dur by the student leader organizations that constantly filled the streets of Jakarta pushing for Gus Dur to resign. At first the Gus Dur supporters just watched and kept their patience. But after a while the demonstrations actually formed public opinion and created a notion reflected by the press— including international media—that Gus Dur indeed had no support. This made his supporters at grassroots level lose their patience. Angered, they went to the streets in East Java to demonstrate support for him.

These demonstrations in East Java were portrayed in the press as being totally different from the demonstrations against Gus Dur in Jakarta. While the Jakarta demonstrations were painted as being the honest expression of free thought, those in East Java were branded as the work of fanatics out to disturb the peace. There was one incident that contributed to this image, the demonstration against the provincial office of Golkar in Surabaya. A large number of people demonstrated in front of the building and it seemed that eventually some managed to slip through and set the building on fire. It was put out quite early so no extensive damage was done, but damage was done to the image of Gus Dur supporters. They were seen as being violent, burning down buildings and intolerant of opposition.

All through that time Gus Dur was making constant telephone calls to East Java and to leaders of the political groups that supported him. I listened in on the conversations to some of his telephone contacts, and the theme was constant. Gus Dur asked them not to create trouble in the streets. If they had to demonstrate, he explained, do it peacefully because if they were to get involved in violence it would actually damage his presidency. It would deny the Gus Dur tradition of nonviolence. I heard this over and over again, and the culmination came when tens of thousands of people finally came to Jakarta. After much deliberation, they agreed to have a mass prayer instead of a street demonstration. Still there was considerable public concern even about holding a mass prayer and publications like *Newsweek* and television networks like CNN had the time of their lives building up tension for that mass prayer on 30 March. They speculated that the prayers would turn into street demonstrations and that Jakarta would not be safe. So convincing were the false alarms by these publications that people disappeared from the street. Some even left the city on that weekend and a few foreign governments issued travel advisories recommending people not to come to Indonesia at that time. That was a ridiculous statement considering the size of Indonesia. Even in Jakarta any effect of that meeting would be confined to a half-kilometer radius. Nevertheless, public opinion formed against the peaceful intentions of Gus Dur.

We tried to explain the incident in East Java when the Golkar office burned down, because we found out from police reports and from independent observations that actually Gus Dur supporters had never even entered the building. Even more telling, at the start of the demonstration the building had already been infiltrated by people who did not belong to groups supporting Gus Dur. It was these people who came in ahead of the demonstration to start a fire. That is a very familiar technique used in public disturbances. Ever since I can remember, somebody would burn down buildings and put the blame on the legitimate demonstrators. This happened in the 1974 Malari incident, when shops at Pasar Senen in Jakarta were burned down to discredit the student movement. You also had people burning down a shopping mall in Banjarmasin during the 1997 elections, and in Jakarta to discredit people who were campaigning in the 1999 election. Of course the infamous 1998 May Riots clearly had burnings, lootings and rapes that were not committed by demonstrators seeking reform. Likewise in East Java, the destruction of Golkar's office was *not* done by the people supporting Gus Dur, but quite possibly by those who were trying to discredit the movement.

We were quite apprehensive as we neared the *Istighotsah* (mass prayer) in Jakarta on 29 March. We were dead

certain that the PKB, NU, Ansor, all the organizations
that supported Gus Dur did not have violence in mind.
But who knows, we thought, somebody might again try
to discredit them. Fortunately this time, everything was
under control. The mass prayers were conducted
peacefully involving a huge crowd of at least three
hundred thousand filling up the Senayan parking
grounds behind the Hilton. For some inexplicable reason
CNN reported the number as fifty thousand. Other
foreign publications reported the crowd to be anywhere
from twenty to one hundred thousand strong. At the
other extreme, some enthusiasts came up with higher
estimates.

From my personal experience in estimating crowds,
three hundred thousand would be the closest approx-
imation. All you have to do is look at the TV footage of
the events in the Senayan parking lot complex. You would
probably agree if you go over to the huge parking lot which
is often used as a parade ground. There were hundreds of
thousands people praying, reflecting, meeting each other,
congratulating each other, giving support but not doing
anything remotely violent. The only physical incident I
saw was when a European reporter fainted in the heat of
the late morning. Most of the people went home to their
provinces right after the event, going straight from the
assembly to the railway station in a huge convoy of buses.
I felt a great lightening of my mental burden, knowing
that I was on the right side with these people, who did not
just preach anti-violence but also showed the world to have
faith in their strong record of nonviolence. I shrugged with
resignation when the foreign media refused to acknow-
ledge this victory of peace and stubbornly kept up their
dogged slant against Gus Dur.

If people really knew Gus Dur and his traditions, they would not be so arbitrary as to associate Gus Dur with any brand of violence. Gus Dur is not a newcomer to public life. He has been in the spotlight for over thirty years. His organization NU has been active for more than eighty years and is known for its moderate and tolerant stance. The foreign media who injected the flavor of violence into Gus Dur's image did their profession a disservice and betrayed the public trust. I am glad that now, after everything is seen in perspective, many have altered their position and some actually have expressed regrets over their misperception. But at that time, it did do a lot of damage, it did make people impatient with President Wahid, and it did get his legitimate government out of power.

Reform invites Reaction

For months we were kept on the defensive: explaining the president to the press, correcting factual errors, exposing abusive misrepresentation. In the end I understood the adage 'the people will believe any lie if you repeat it often enough'. Some of us decided to be more assertive and fight for the truth. When Memorandum I came out, we happened to have a cabinet meeting scheduled afterwards. Actually political matters were never given too much time in the official deliberations of the government. But in that cabinet meeting the security briefing touched on the matter of political opposition and so we found ourselves discussing Memorandum I and how to deal with it. It was the Coordinating Minister for the Economy Rizal Ramli, possessing a strong background in practical politics from his student days, who voiced a suggestion that he had discussed with me earlier. I thought it was the correct position to take. Which is, when we are

attacked without strong legal substance, then it is proper
to take the matter to the public. Rizal said that now is the
time that we have to win the hearts of the public. The
politicians will never be persuaded as it was a matter that
cut across their political interests, but the people will want
to hear what we have to say.

I never spoke up at cabinet meetings, but nodded
silent agreement and slipped Rizal a note supporting his
position. The discussion went on along those lines. People
who were not of the same political persuasion as Rizal and
myself thought it would invite political opposition and
political trouble. There were two types of people who held
that belief: the first type actually wanted to stay away from
political controversy and the second type actually wanted
to stay away from a sharper line for the government. But
I knew what Rizal meant, and I was happy to hear him
explain that the only way to win the hearts of the public at
that point was to show ourselves as being firmly on the
side of reform by implementing very strong anti-
corruption measures, putting names to the justice process,
and being very strong on security issues—in other words
moving away from the compromise position that had been
dogging us since the first coalition cabinet. This clearly
divided the cabinet even more, although nobody spoke
up for the other side. So the matter was left unresolved
since the president said that there was no need for the
government to take a political position in any case. These
thoughts were just a topic of discussion and as president
he would have the sole responsibility of responding
politically.

After the meeting, I asked Gus Dur whether I could
announce to the press that the president has now "decided
to engage of reform without compromise." I loved that

phrase, and as the president agreed to it, I used it in the press conference. I said the president had been trying very hard to speed up the reform process, getting the attorney general to look into violations of corruption laws, urging the human rights groups to look into violations of human rights, but so far we have not met the success we needed. Furthermore, the political support we expected from Parliament was not forthcoming, and in fact Parliament was taking the opposite stance to the president on other trivial non-issues like Bulogate and Bruneigate. So I said, in order to get the focus of the country back onto the matters that concern its citizens, the president has stated that he will engage the government in a program of reform without compromise, i.e. taking a tougher stance on corruption and human rights violations.

The press liked this stance as well and it got good publicity— right up to the moment when some reporters went to the office of Minister Susilo Bambang Yudhoyono searching for more quotes. Susilo Bambang said, "there was no cabinet decision on the program for 'reform without compromise'. I think the presidential spokesman did not speak on the basis of the cabinet decision." So the reporters came back to me and compared his statements to mine, looking for inconsistencies. Of course, it was not inconsistent because what Susilo Bambang said was true: there was no cabinet decision, but I was not referring to that. I was referring instead to the president's direction, to his intention to engage in a program of reform without compromise. That represented a political intention which was not necessarily readily translatable into a cabinet decision. In any case, according to the constitution, the cabinet is a technical body responsible for implementing the policies of the president.

Right after this gathered steam, we saw the opposition harden and the people behind the memorandum process complain that instead of the president listening to the memorandum and moving closer to Parliament, now he was moving further away and resorting to extreme measures, to which I responded, "How can you question a decision to take a firmer stance on corruption and human rights violations? How you can have *any* arguments with that? That is actually the mandate which was given to the president!" From then on we didn't engage in debate and we stood firm on our stand of reform without compromise. Unfortunately on the political front, this eroded the president's support base even more. The reason, we were beginning to realize and see with utmost clarity, is that the Parliament, the Assembly, and the rest of the political system are dominated by people who did have some corruption issues, some skeletons in their closet. And of course people who were involved in human rights violations were not at all keen on the idea of reform without compromise.

Breakfast with Wolves

My wife never finished watching "Dances With Wolves," a big Kevin Costner movie in 1991. The movie starts out gently but ends up quite violently—and my wife couldn't bear to sit through the horrifying ending. Fortunately it was never like that in my time with President Wahid, but we did have many breakfast meetings which set me thinking about whether it would all lead to something tragic. At issue was a hot discussion topic introduced by the president on the options we should explore if the constitution were to be endangered by unconstitutional political acts of Parliament. The topic came up at the time the weekly breakfast meetings were started.

Gus Dur is a man who loves to meet people, and sees absolutely no reason to exclude anyone from a good discussion. He disregards protocol and does not mind meeting people wherever they happen to live or wherever they happen to work. So breakfast is open season for discussion. This style of Gus Dur then took shape in a little tradition which Gus Dur started and Megawati ended. At first they took place over breakfasts in the palace and hosted by the president, then later the vice president and the president took turns. Finally they came to be held every week at the vice president's official residence. I suspect there wasn't anything sinister behind the permanent change of venues, but I do think it might have had something to do with the fact that the food at Megawati's home is immeasurably better than the cuisine in the palace.

I would have to look in somebody's archives to see when these meetings started exactly, but it must have been around the time that the special committee (Pansus) of Parliament was preparing Memorandum I. The breakfast meetings were designed to discuss comprehensive topics on security issues. However, invariably the talk would drift toward anticipation of the political crisis which could come out from the impasse of the Parliament with the president.

The Wednesday breakfast meetings were always interesting and quite pleasant. The military presence unmistakably defined the purpose of the meeting. But everybody was behaving in a civil and informal way and to top it all, we always enjoyed Megawati's famous breakfasts. She is really fantastic with food and these meals were always multi-track affairs. One track for porridge and accessories, another one for fried rice, and the third track is for the adventurous: whatever ethnic food or

Mahfud MD, the outspoken and smart minister of defense, with Marzuki Darusman, master politician turned inscrutable attorney general.

special breakfast happens to be in the imagination of the vice presidential kitchen.

Due diligence was always afforded to general security matters. After breakfast each person would give his account on the current status of the security situation, especially in Aceh, Central Kalimantan, the Maluku, Irian Jaya, and in the urban centers.

This was a very select group of people. Beside the president and vice president, the standard list included Minister Susilo Bambang Yudhoyono, Commander of the Indonesian Armed Forces Admiral Widodo, the Chief of Staff of each branch of the military and the Chief of the Police, General Bimantoro. You would also always have the head of intelligence, General Ari Kumaat. And then you have the Minister of Defense, Mahfud MD, the cabinet secretary, Marsillam Simandjuntak and myself.

Nothing was ever discussed in a controversial manner in these meetings, but as far as the public was concerned these meetings were thought to be deeply controversial, either because of the spin the press put on it, or by the remarks of some of the attendants of the meeting that were issued to the press later on.

The most controversial issue arising from this meeting was the decree which Gus Dur had suggested might have to be put into effect if the constitution were threatened. And by that he meant that if Parliament goes headlong into its conspiracy against the Office of the President, then it would tread into dangerous ground by threatening the constitution. President Wahid proposed that if it ever got out of hand, then he might have to safeguard the constitution and declare a state of emergency, suspend Parliament and call for fresh elections. Every time he brought this up as a topic of discussion, nobody would respond. Even when they were directly asked, they *still* did not respond—least of all the vice president. But outside of the meeting comments adverse to the president's proposal would fill up the papers. This happened again, again and again.

These meetings generally were supposed to provide political consensus on security matters and also a bridge of understanding between elements of the military and the police and the civilian government. I don't know how much they actually achieved because the negative spin resulting from the meetings exceeded whatever understanding could have been gained. Especially since nobody really talked except the president. The others either voiced no opinion or responded through different channels such as the media and by leaks to people outside. The meetings did more damage than good because it exposed the president's suggestions in a twisted manner.

Media reports did not reflect the sincerity of his calls for discussion, and the new political culture of openness

President Wahid was trying to introduce. Sadly, the meetings were not used by the vice president to contribute to the political dialogue. In fact, she was absent for the last few sessions. We would still have the meetings in her official residence on Jalan Teuku Umar but she would not be there. She always had someone prepare the delicious breakfasts, though.

The problem of dealing with the unconstitutional tendencies in Parliament was left unaddressed in these breakfast meetings. As parliamentary politics degraded to abusive levels the president sought various means to prevent Parliament from transgressing its constitutional boundaries. When efforts to find a compromise failed and there was no choice but to issue the decree, President Wahid selflessly bore the responsibility himself with no reference to any of the breakfast participants.

Bangkok with Thaksin

I welcomed the trip to Thailand as a change of pace. To me this seemed like trying a long pass when our ground game was getting nowhere. In May 2001 Thaksin Shinawatra had just been elected Prime Minister of Thailand when we got feelers from Bangkok offering a bilateral summit meeting between Thaksin and Gus Dur. It was to be a warm meeting with substance, and it had to be done quickly. Both sides had to gain from the economic agreements being prepared and politically it also would strengthen both governments in their respective countries.

Around this time there was another major outbreak of fighting in Aceh. It appeared to involve weapons and people who are thought to have gained international passage through some intermediary points in southern Thailand. This was to be a prime subject for discussion, and as it turned out the Thai government was extremely cooperative in investigations into these suspicions. We also needed an agreement on fisheries to deal with the many Thai fisherman who were caught in Indonesian waters and the Wahid government's pragmatic position was that to attempt to eradicate illegal fishing would be an exercise in futility. The agreement basically covered divisions on gains made from such illegal fishing which would be later ratified by each government. But this was all in the initial stage. There were also initial-stage documents dealing with natural gas exploration and the field of internet technology. In the case of the internet technology, this was to be completed with the ASEAN Institute of Technology, where Gus Dur made an academic address on a previous visit during Prime Minister Chuan Leekpai's term, when Gus Dur was honored with an honorary doctorate from the AIT.

Thailand's PM Thaksin Shinawatra managed to arrange a warm welcome and come to substantial security and economic agreements with the Indonesian government on an intensively prepared one-day working visit to Bangkok.

The one-day visit of President Wahid to Thailand resulted in a number of economic agreements, including refining Indonesian crude oil by Thailand. It was good that Indonesia could utilize the excess capacity of Thailand's refinery facilities for our crude oil. Indonesian refinery capacity is less than our domestic requirements. The cooperation in the fuel sector could have made a big difference, and it was only one of six agreements made during Gus Dur's visit. Other agreements were made in fishery, trade, aviation, tourism and natural rubber. Prime Minister Thaksin and Gus Dur told a news conference that an agreement had been reached in principle to refine about 200,000 barrels of Indonesian oil a day.

Before Gus Dur's visit, Coordinating Minister for Economic Affairs Rizal Ramli had discussed the issue with Thaksin and a number of Thai economic ministers. Ramli visited the country on 29 April after the Thaksin connection was established through close personal friends of Gus Dur who had joined the Thaksin government. The nature of their relationship was such that the important state visit was planned in just a couple of weeks. I was personally involved in the preparation and communications, which made me hostage of the cellphone and e-mail continuously. Rizal was busy with other important things including IMF negotiations, and by the time the visit happened he was not around so I did the informal work in the economic agreements. It was an exhausting visit because I had to double up both as spokesman as well as deal with some of the substance of the economic deals being prepared by the two governments. This no doubt contributed to my collapse the day after we returned home.

Economic Minister Rizal Ramli downloaded his points before he had to leave me in Bangkok to work on the economic agreement with Thailand's Thaksin government.

Coming back to Jakarta, I was equipped with success stories on the economic front to show the Indonesian and international press that, while they were really heating up the political news and rounding up momentum for impeachment, President Wahid was staying above the battle and moving the economic ship along.

Unfortunately the press were too blinded by 'hot political news' to see the significance of this visit. While I used all my energy to elaborate on the economic successes of the trip, the domestic press kept harping on the question of Parliament versus the president, and other gossip that they wanted to nail on Gus Dur. Oh well. I came home from the press briefing at Halim Airport exhausted and not feeling so well. I had missed out on quite a lot of sleep during my days in Bangkok, tired from filling in on work outside my own brief. In the interest of economizing, the presidential delegation shared rooms at the Bangkok Hilton. I was lucky to be assigned to Colonel Muhadi as my roommate, head of the security forces section directly responsible for the president's safety. Being in the same room as *Pak* Muhadi made me feel safe but still I could not stretch out or snore as freely as I would if I were alone. I had a fitful sleep on 16 May 2001.

Near-Death Experience

On 17 May 2001 I had a heart failure which brought me close to death. At least that is what the doctors said. In fact, I must have died for several seconds, losing my pulse and my heart rate for an instant. Luckily I was in the emergency room of Pondok Indah Hospital at that time and the excellent care provided by the ambulance crew, emergency room paramedics and doctors was able to revive me and put me on the road to a very speedy recovery. The heart failure happened at home after eating rather a lot of sashimi with my sons and grand niece, taking a break after the strenuous trip to Bangkok and a morning session at a seminar. Eleven years before I had an optional cardiac bypass. Whilst I had not suffered a heart attack, a routine check up revealed that I needed a heart bypass. So I had it done by the late Dr. Victor Chang at St Vincent's Hospital in Sydney.

Things went well for eleven years. My weight was not good but I was always active playing tennis and taking the occasionally walk. But when I joined President Wahid, I lost all my exercise time and instead sat around and ate a lot. I gained so much weight that strangers commented I kept getting bigger and bigger on television. I became very passive physically. That was a great burden on my heart and the last straw came on that fateful day of 17 May when I had to be rushed off to the emergency room gasping for breath.

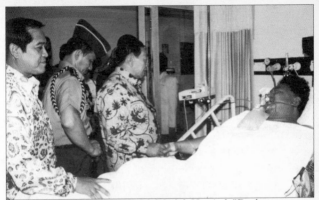

Intensive Care Unit at Pondok Indah Hospital. "Don't worry about anything except getting well," he told me.

Since my release from the hospital I have been exercising a lot. I started off walking three kilometers every day and now I swim one hour (about a thousand meters) every day. I do floor exercises and some lifting with weights trying to develop a good body. My diet has gone well and at the time this book went to press I had lost twenty kilograms from my pre-hospital weight. In dieting and in politics, it is a strong will that makes the difference. After two weeks in the hospital and a month of home recuperation, I reported back for duty although Gus Dur advised me to take it easy. My health seemed more important to him than my work contribution. At this time the president was quite active going around town visiting various people who had a hand in influencing the politics of presidential impeachment. As I had the energy to do so, I joined him on some of his rounds.

The House Across From the Mosque

There is a house on an expensive street in Kebayoran, one of the upper-class suburbs of Jakarta. It is just across the street from a famous mosque. The house, grand in the Dutch-Indonesian fifties style, is owned by an old friend of mine, a fun guy who made it big in the free-wheeling real estate deals of the seventies, being a protégé of the West Java military and political elite. By the nineties he was maturing from a *bon vivant* to a political figure, becoming a major Golkar official when others of his generation were fading out. That house is just one of many he owns, and is practically dedicated to the political lobbying that is the trademark of Golkar.

Early in my career as a television entertainer and a public commentator, my friend had often urged me to come by to the house and, in his words, have a chat with the boys. Although we were good 'hi buddy' friends, I never accepted his invitation because it wasn't my style in that political climate to spend an evening talking politics, business or other useful stuff—I greatly preferred to be home watching television or taking a nap.

But finally I came to that house in 1998 during Habibie's time as president. Things were moving. The public was heavily scrutinizing the Bank Bali scandal, which involved a hundred times more money as the Bulogate scandal. The case actually came close to resolution. The major players had already been identified including names like Central Bank Governor Sjahril Sabirin, Minister for State Enterprises Tanri Abeng and Chairman of the Supreme Advisory Council A.A. Baramuli, and State Secretary Muladi who heavily denied involvement. They all came from the Golkar party. It was depressing to see how much corruption was a part of the government in those times. Later on I thought it was ironic that President Wahid's government was sullied by corruption charges when there was nothing even suggested that was on the scale of what his accusers got away with.

The activists assembled in the House Across From the Mosque were eagerly on the reform side. They were rivals of Golkar's Habibie and people who had left Golkar. The spirit of adventure made exposing corruption scandals quite exciting. They consorted with anti-corruption groups which made the whole thing politically correct. From the data we saw that there was enough to go for the kill. The purpose of the meeting was to plan what should be done in public and in Parliament to make sure the legal process against the Bank Bali scandal would proceed. I was invited because of my media knowledge. The political significance of 'Baligate' to these politicians was the potential exposure of people like Muladi, Tanri Abeng, and Baramuli. It would surely incriminate President Habibie and ensure the impossibility of his election.

As fate would have it, Habibie's election became an impossibility for reasons other than Baligate. So the motion against Tanri Abeng, Muladi and Baramuli stopped when Habibie was replaced. People found other things to do, especially Marzuki Darusman who became the attorney general and turned soft. Arifin Panigoro, who was supporting the Indonesian Corruption Watch at that time later did not find it important to go further against the corruption scandal, turning instead against President Wahid whose government was threatening him for his own affairs. Later, Tanri Abeng tried to regain respectability and even published an expensive book on privatization although he was indicted in two corruption cases.

The actual point of the story is that the House Across From the Mosque has seen quite interesting things in its day. My second contact with that house was when my car got a flat tire right in front of its driveway, and I left it there for the night while I rushed off in a taxi to catch an appointment. It must have fueled speculation for I was the presidential spokesman at that time. People must have thought I spent the night at the home of a Golkar leader when Golkar had morphed back into a protector of the New Order. The third encounter was the really interesting meeting, with a totally different cast of characters and issues.

The Supposedly Secret Meeting

Saturdays were optional for work. There were usually no essential presidential programs, except for some events of protocol. The president had never prescribed working hours for me. He just left it entirely up to me to decide when to be around him and when not to be. And I used this freedom to take Saturdays as a day of rest from routine presidential work. Instead I would use Saturdays to meet with reporters or write or attend meetings, but I would generally be away from the palace. But not on this particular Saturday, which was not long after I was back into my daily schedule.

I was informed by Greg Barton that the president was going to visit Pramoedya Ananta Toer at his home somewhere outside Bogor. I thought this was too interesting to miss. Two of the great cultural icons of Indonesia were about to meet, one a president and the other one a former political prisoner on the island of Buru for a decade and in his house for two—and also a great literary figure. In fact he has been nominated several times for the Nobel Prize in Literature. So I decided to would go along with the president on this trip and I informed him I would be there on Saturday.

Having just come out from my recuperation period I had no idea of the background of this meeting. I learned later that the visit to Pramoedya's home was related to the president's schedule. It was Saturday 7 July 2001. The president was to hold a much-heralded meeting with heads of the major political parties at the Bogor presidential palace. As political collision approach-ed, cloak-and-dagger political maneuvers rose to a fever pitch. There were endless permutations of possible deals as the forces against Abdurrahman Wahid started to do their own calculations based on their particular interests. The thing about a multiparty system is that without a clear majority, ethics are the only limits to possible coalitions. And ethics were the one commodity that was in short supply among Indonesia's politicians. "Who, who, who? Who's the slayer? Who's the victim? Who's on my side?" my brother Luki used to recite when I was in grade school. That line was perfect for these times. Was Megawati still committed to Gus Dur? Or would she consider teaming up with Akbar Tandjung's Golkar? She cannot possibly be accepted by Hamzah Haz's conservative party who were adamant in their opposition to a female president. Think again. What about PAN and Amien Rais? Well, they were the ones who made Gus Dur president, and look what they are doing now.

When I was in the hospital I heard vaguely of deals being made and compromises being hammered out. Akbar Tandjung of Golkar seemed to be open to a deal to keep the Wahid presidency from falling. Yet some of their actions belie that promise. As I stepped out from the isolation of the sickbed I was immediately sucked into the political whirlpool. So there I was, preparing to visit Pramoedya as the political waters swirled all around us. It was swirling so fast that the big meeting in Bogor had actually been called off and Gus Dur no longer needed to go to Bogor. But it is again proof of Gus Dur's typical sincerity he did not cancel the visit to Pramoedya . He traveled the sixty kilometers with great purpose and enjoyment. In fact, it was only when I was writing these words that I realized that the Pramoedya visit was not the intended highlight of the day. But then in a larger sense, the Gus Dur-Pramoedya meeting was much more significant than party politics. Quite apart from Gus Dur's personal admiration for Pramoedya, as president he was paying the tribute of a nation to a much-maligned cultural icon who had suffered so much with such elegance, emerging now to take his rightful place as a defining symbol of Indonesia's resilience.

After an hour-long private chat, Gus Dur took his leave and Pramoedya was left to deal with the press horde crowded around the front of his house. When the press asked Pramoedya for comment he said, "We had a private discussion and I wish it to remain that way. But I will tell you I told Gus Dur that under no circumstances should he step down. The New Order is vying for power again and he is the only one who can stand up to it."

What was really interesting on that day with Pramoedya was what happened before the visit. I had come to Merdeka Palace at 8 o'clock for the 9 o'clock trip. Colonel Sabar Yudho, the presidential aide, informed me that the president would attend a 'secret' meeting first before he went to Pramoedya's house. I asked who would attend the 'secret' meeting. Sabar paused and shrugged, "Well, for you it's not a secret. He is seeing Akbar Tandjung." At the moment the president emerged from his office and I asked him about the 'secret' meeting and where should I meet him afterwards in order to catch the trip to visit

Pramoedya. And he said, "You just come along, it's alright." It was great to be here on this Saturday. Free time filled with interesting programs, I thought.

Akbar Tandjung was a crucial player whose Golkar party held the second-largest number of seats. Between Golkar and Megawati's PDI-P—the largest party in Parliament—they could decide which way things would go. As Megawati became more and more of an enigma and increasingly inaccessible to the president, Akbar Tandjung had become politically acceptable. Besides, Akbar is a person of great political competence. He is a skilled communicator with extensive experience in political negotiations. He can give lengthy statements without committing himself. Akbar is always ready with a deal, survivor of thirty-some years of Indonesian politics. I had known Akbar since we were both student activists. He was in Jakarta while I was in Bandung.

I rode in the back seat with the president in his limousine, and lo and behold, we drove right to the House Across From the Mosque. As I expected a secret and private meeting with just Akbar, I was quite surprised to find a group of people waiting for us—and they were just as surprised to see me. So, maybe it was more of a surprise meeting than a secret one.

From the Golkar side there was Akbar Tandjung and Marzuki Darusman. The president came with me and later Alwi Shihab joined us. The ironic thing is that my side were new acquaintances while the other side consisted of friends I had known from thirty years back. Everybody did their best at social chit-chat and Akbar Tandjung said to Gus Dur, "Gus, do you know that I visited Wimar in the hospital?" Characteristically Gus Dur replied, "Of

course, everybody visited him." Then Gus Dur immediately got down to business. It was very brief, because
all Gus Dur said was, "Well, if my understanding of the
report is correct, then we are all in full agreement. Let's
avoid the dramatics. Now it is time for your people to sit
down and work out the text of the joint communiqué
which will be issued by the political leaders."

Marzuki and Akbar agreed to that and so did Alwi.
I just sat there and smiled. Marzuki wanted to go into the
specifics of the joint communiqué to which Gus Dur just
shrugged his shoulders and said, "It's OK, whatever you
decide. You know what my main points are: I can not
betray the constitution and I have to have the final say
over all appointments at the cabinet level."

With that meeting most of the tension disappeared.
Then all speculated as to whether Hamzah Haz and
Megawati would agree. Akbar said, "I'm sure Hamzah
Haz would agree." Gus Dur had the same opinion on
Hamzah Haz. As long as his personal demands were met,
Hamzah would agree to just about anything. At the top
of Hamzah's list that he be given a position of importance
in the top level of the government, whether in the cabinet
or in an extra-cabinet position like Chairman of the State
Audit Agency. As for Megawati, nobody was quite sure
what she wanted. But Akbar said, "Well, if Megawati
doesn't sign, it's OK, we can go ahead with just the three
of us." So it was agreed that the four leaders would convene
at the Bogor Palace the following day, Sunday.

The full implications of that meeting did not dawn on me
until months after President Wahid had been ousted from
office. In hindsight President Wahid was attending the
meeting to confirm a political compromise that had been

negotiated earlier. Having just returned from two months of hospitalization and home rest, I had no knowledge of the deal. Apparently the agreement was to be announced at the meeting of the party leaders in Bogor. This was supposedly designed to deflate the possibility of impeachment. Akbar Tandjung at that time posed as a moderate who announced the inadvisability. That was not in the mind of the Senayan Cowboys like Arifin Panigoro and the Central Axis firebrands.

Marzuki Darusman, Deputy Chairman of Golkar, was a member of Gus Dur's cabinet as Attorney General. He always proclaimed his loyalty to Gus Dur. So here we had Marzuki Darusman who is loyal to Gus Dur, we had Akbar Tandjung who voices support for Gus Dur, Gus Dur himself was there as well as Alwi Shihab, his right hand man. It was quite interesting to hear Akbar speak because he was more or less providing the substance of the meeting. From the way he spoke, it seemed the only thing left to do for a political compromise was to draw up a joint resolution. There were some questions to which we still had to get the views of Megawati, and we knew how to handle Hamzah.

The meeting adjourned on a positive note. Maybe this is what Akbar meant when he visited me in the hospital after my heart failure several weeks before. I had been put on a news embargo and had gone five weeks without political news. I was woken up from my afternoon nap by Akbar shaking me gently and saying: "Wim… Wim…." I thought I was in another world as his face filled up the screen of my slowly focusing vision. Just as I came out of my stupor I heard his voice drone, "You know, I was with the boys and I told them not to push forward with the Assembly special session (which could lead to

Akbar Tandjung, Parliament speaker, head of Soeharto-founded Golkar party. Good friend, professional politican, hard to figure out.

impeachment). Is that not a good thing?" What? Who? I thought. Sure, impeachment is not a good thing. Hey, where are the nurses? Then fully awake, I listened to Akbar explain that he had come from a meeting where he succeeded in convincing people not to push for the special session. So I thought my weeks away from work had done the president some good. Hearing Akbar speak so comfortingly I thought everything was fine, although some thoughts were still nagging me.

    A few hours later I sneaked a peek at the evening news, something I was not allowed to do at that time. But Akbar's sudden visit had aroused my curiosity and I sat up when I saw him answering questions to a crowd of reporters, still wearing the same suit in which he came to see me. To my amazement I heard him say, "Well, I think we at Parliament feel the special session is unavoidable." I sank back into my pillow and decided not to worry about it. But I could not help thinking why he should mislead a guy who is confined to a hospital bed. Maybe he wanted to make me comfortable. Maybe he thought I might call someone. Or maybe it was just a habit to say things, or maybe his deal did not work out. It could be all of them, but I was not too surprised. Knowing Akbar, this was just one of the many twists and turns which have made me give up trying to believe him. And I did not tell anyone about this for a long time.

History now tells that everything discussed in that secret meeting fell through: no compromise, no word from Megawati or anyone as the political field officers chopped up the presidency of Indonesia. There was even a statement from Akbar Tandjung on television that he had met with the president in a private meeting. Well, so the meeting was not that secret after all.

Choosing sides

There were very many good guys and just a few bad guys. But most of the good guys did not take risks when they were called on to do so. The ministers in President Wahid's cabinet were mostly good people, far better in ethics and integrity than in any cabinet in the last few decades. Only a few stood out for unethical behavior precisely because they were the exceptions. But in the moment of truth as Gus Dur received the final political blows from his political foes, many shrunk from their previous courageous positions. The disappointing behavior showed up in recalcitrance to support the president and politicking for individual exit scenarios which did not help Gus Dur in the last moments of his presidency. When people look for the Judas in the story of Gus Dur's downfall it is difficult because there were so many different candidates. Megawati succeeded Gus Dur as president without being portrayed as the prime perpetrator of a betrayal. So people missed the signs of disloyalty among cabinet officers which took form in undue closeness to the vice president as the president became isolated. It was a sign of the scramble for safety that when Gus Dur came back from his brief trip to the States after he stepped down, that no cabinet minister except Sarwono Kusumaatmadja showed up to welcome him.

I will not comment much on Parliament members who threw all ethics to the wind when they went on a rampage against President Wahid. Perhaps they regretted it afterwards because in the weeks after their successful conspiracy they did not attempt to set any new directions for the country. The Megawati government has been left to drift without the benefit of parliamentary guidance. It confirms my feeling that the basis of the anti-Gus Dur movement in Parliament was purely power politics. Probably the most serious damage to the nation's political life is not that they violated the public trust in an innocent president, but that they did it for nothing except ego and greed.

It always feels good that outside of these few characters who lost their balance because of the sudden change in political climate, many individuals stand straight as icons of a new society. No matter that they are outside positions of power and responsibility at the moment. A nation cannot go wrong if it has people like Munir, the human rights activist, Hendardi, the tireless defendant of civil rights, Luhut Pangaribuan, the lawyer with integrity, Jaya Suprana, the intellectual and entertainer, and Karlina Leksono and Esther I. Yusuf, the gentle proponents of the fierce battle against violence and discrimination. Countless others make up the Hall of Fame in the first few years of Indonesia's flawed transition. They have different

Lunch during cabinet meetings was brief but relaxed, especially at the table with the president, VP and key ministers.

viewpoints on the Gus Dur presidency, but they are untouchable in their integrity and commitment to a better society. They are a picture of an Indonesia that might have been had Gus Dur been more successful in mobilizing political support. And they are still the future of Indonesia. The 'Prague Spring' of democracy was not so much stopped by his enemies, as it was by the failure of friends who could not manage to separate the good from the bad. These might seem like high-flying words but they are necessary to keep our perspective as we go into the story of how the Wahid presidency collapsed.

The Princess Leaves Her Mentor

There was no way President Wahid could have been ousted if Vice President Megawati did not step over to the side of his enemies. For a long time I thought that the Wahid-Megawati team, the nation's biggest political partnership, would carry the game and would overcome all the challenges. But apparently the match made in heaven was destroyed in the Parliament Building. The rupture was caused by personal and political ambitions of many politicians. But the basic differences between Megawati Soekarnoputri and Gus Dur are significant.

Some of these are apparent: Megawati's national-ism, ethnicism, militarism, bureaucracy, and obsession with privacy may be juxtaposed to Gus Dur's respect for the individual, pluralism, human rights, and openness—revealing vast differences between the cultural make-up of these two people. Gus Dur has a rich history of being a man of Islamic and international culture, and was brought up to play a public role. Megawati had no such preparation except to be the daughter of the internationally-known Soekarno, from which she probably cultivated feelings of entitlement similar to scions of famous people.

I came to my job with a desire to work with Vice President Megawati, especially as I had been asked—before my recruitment by President Wahid—by some of her people to consider the possibility of acting as a director of communications for Megawati when it was clear that she would be running the day-to-day functions of the presidency after the August 2000 Assembly session. I had a positive attitude towards her function in Indonesia's mass-based politics and I could accept her as she was. Hence on the first day at work I went up to meet her at lunch. It was at the State Palace where the group of tough parliamentarians had come to be embarrassed by AM Fatwa's tongue-lashing of President Wahid. At lunch time I introduced myself to Megawati, and she said, "Yes, of course I know you," and I said, "I am introducing myself basically as spokesman for the presidency. If you so wish,

Madame, I would like to be of help to you as well." I really meant this because I wanted to see the duo, this team of Gus Dur and Mega, grow as a strong pair. In response to my question as to how I should go about seeing her, Megawati pointed to a man in a neat suit with a very serious face standing in the background who turned out to be Bambang Kesowo, now apparently running the Megawati presidency. At that time Bambang was the secretary for the vice presidential office, and Megawati referred me to him on the matter of how I could best serve the vice president as well as the president. Bambang showed politeness and gave general comments without too much enthusiasm, which I learned is not only the style, but also the substance of this man.

Several days later, we were together with Megawati, her husband Taufik Kiemas, and various high-level officials at Halim Airport. We were waiting for President Wahid to come and begin his journey to Langkawi, Malaysia. Taufik—who is a very friendly, ebullient sort of man—expressed concern that Gus Dur needed stronger press representation and he said that he was very happy to have me on the job. I said, "Yes, I am happy to be here," and then, "I would be happy to be of service to your wife, to the vice president, if she so wishes." Taufik replied, "Now that is a terrific idea!" and with great enthusiasm he brought me to his wife. Megawati said again, "Yes, fine. Let him talk to Bambang Kesowo." And I said, "I already have, Madam. Now I would like to have a meeting with you." "Oh yes, of course. Just leave your name with my aide." Then Taufik took me to the aide and said, "OK, schedule a meeting for Mr Witoelar with Vice President Megawati." The aide said, "Yes, Sir!" took out his notebook and scribbled something. Well, nothing was ever heard since that request for an appointment, so it was another dead end in my quest to communicate with Megawati. After a while, I just gave up trying.

Over my ten months as presidential spokesman I met Megawati quite often but we never had a serious conversation. At the most, our conversations were friendly chit-chat and more often than not the talk revolved around food. She and I are great fans of food, and at that time I was not on diet so I indulged in everything. She has a remarkable knowledge of the availabilities of various kinds of street foods like specialty fried rice, noodles, chicken porridge, lamb *saté* and other Indonesian delicacies. And she knows exactly which corner of the streets of Jakarta, Bogor or Bandung offer the best delicacies.

The other forum in which I met Megawati would be in cabinet meetings where she would preside in session, generally keeping track of time while making sure everybody speaks their minds. In some instances she might moderate some back-and-forth discussion between various ministers. But I never did see her in troubleshooting or problem-solving capacities because I did not attend the working session of the sub-cabinet portfolios which she also chaired as a matter of routine.

The other occasions with the vice president would be in small meetings with the president and one or two ministers and high officials at the Bina Graha building but again, no substance could be detected from her role in these conversations. Gus Dur would use his casual style of speech and get down to the subject at hand. He rarely changed this style in the various meetings that he attended. But Megawati would be quite formal and only respond with a smile and a nod of polite acquiescence. Sometimes she would make a vague comment but never raise any questions and certainly never enter into a debate of different opinions.

I respected Megawati as a person of social class. She rarely showed emotion and was always very respectful and generous with her famous smile. Like a princess, she maintained an invisible wall that even her closest associates only traverse occasionally. I tried to maintain my casual self with her, but I could never relax completely. Had she not shown political ambition, people could mistake her as a passive princess exacting fealty from her loyal subjects.

My attempts to be friendly with her, at best, would bring gentle acknowledgment and our relations were friendly albeit distant. There was, however, one incident that still makes me smile with embarrassment. It happened one morning before a cabinet meeting as we were moving from the president's office to the cabinet meeting hall. As usual, Gus Dur walked side-by-side next to Megawati. The president was assisted by two aides and Megawati walked alone circled by several people. In a way this move between rooms was always an awkward maneuver. There were too many people trying to walk across the floor at the same time Then everybody had to maintain a level of decorum as this was a formal occasion—in formal attire and all. But the real awkwardness came because both the president and the vice president are not people who are accustomed to moving around with fluid agility. The others in the group are supposed to do their part in keeping the procession moving smoothly. That is where I committed my *faux pas*.

My place has to be as close to the president as I could be whenever reasonably possible so that he could find me at any time. So when the group suddenly scrambled to enter the cabinet room I jumped up trying to catch my place, having been caught away from the group trying to make a call on my mobile phone. I saw the president enter the doorway and hastened to catch up with him. I am a heavy man anyway but at that time I was at my 122-kilogram peak, so it was difficult to maintain and semblance of poise in narrow spaces. Before I knew it, I realized I had bumped into someone, and that the someone was Vice President Megawati. The impact was such that she lost her balance and had to take a few steps sideways to limit the damage. I was very embarrassed and quickly apologized. To her credit she laughed freely and even gave a mock hand movement to punish me. That was my most intimate contact with this inscrutable lady.

Once or twice I saw she had a clear personal position on an issue. One occasion I remember clearly was her action in preparing Gus Dur to face the press in response to the first Memorandum. She worked with me and Minister Susilo Bambang Yudhoyono to prepare a statement of instant response by the president to the censure expressed by Parliament. Her position was that we should avoid putting the president on the spot by antagonizing Parliament. I still do not understand how she moved from that position to one of extreme disloyalty as the parliament juggernaut gained momentum.

Megawati defines her social values and applies them to her task. Abdurrahman always tried to contribute his personal values to social development. His primary values are very clear: peace and democracy. He tried to negotiate with the people of Aceh and of Irian Jaya. He earned friendship and respect from some the secessionist groups. He tried to tackle human rights abuse by defusing the danger in the military by taking out people like General Wiranto, who was alleged to have been one of the biggest abusers. He did all these things based on some simple concepts which people know are good. But he did not have the support from the political system, from friend or foe. He was basically a spearhead without the spear. As such his campaign lost balance and flew in all kinds of directions.

∽∾

The slim political thread which had kept the Gus Dur presidency together was being pulled and twisted in all directions ever since the beginning. When I first joined, Gus Dur's confidence was to me both inspiring and worrying. I admired the fact that he tried to keep the coalition that had been formed by others. It consisted of the Amien Rais group, the Golkar group, the Megawati group and his own group built around NU and PKB.

Even when this coalition produced an ineffective government it was still considered worthwhile, since everybody had a stake in the government. But this kind of stability which was not founded in the actual strength of the government, soon became counter-productive when it became clear government performance had been sacrificed for political unity. In that situation political unity became illusory, clearly a cosmetic covering a very rapidly deteriorating condition. Especially when you add the personal ambition of personalities with their oversized egos, it became clear that the first Wahid-Megawati cabinet was a cabinet of no purpose. This situation was utilized by those seeking to benefit from this uncertainty by weakening Gus Dur's position and strengthening Megawati's position.

Megawati at first resisted the idea of being pushed forward to challenge Gus Dur, but eventually her emotions got the better of her. By August 2000 she had agreed to allow her people to come forward with stronger political positions, in fact stronger than prescribed by the constitution and the rules of the game. Making use of her position as vice president, they invented justification for her to have special powers as if she were a prime minister. The reasons were dubious in legal terms, but gained ground because Gus Dur's government was not perceived to be performing well. The regular spin was that 'Gus Dur is not stable' or 'Gus Dur is mercurial'. They aimed to nominate Megawati under the pretext of providing balance and stability.

The problem was that Megawati encouraged the first signs of strength by the opposition against Gus Dur. Despite her immense popularity she never could find self-confidence, so when Gus Dur reshuffled the cabinet after the Assembly's annual session of August 2000, she got cold feet and did not state her preferences. On the day of the announcement she left after the final meetings and let Gus Dur announce the new cabinet by himself. Megawati's absence was considered significant by the public, but Gus Dur made light of that fact and said in an offhand remark that Megawati had to go home "because she wanted to take a bath." Most of the public reacted to that remark adversely and failed to see the humor in the quote—feeling that Gus Dur had offended Megawati. The story behind the scenes is that after a day of exhausting negotiations it was just a casual remark, perhaps one even implying camaraderie.

The second Gus Dur cabinet which was inaugurated in August 2000 was more homogenous and that was the cabinet that I found when I reported for work in October 2000. I found a cabinet which was working quite well: we had good meetings, good rapport and the spirit of good intentions. Unfortunately, the fact that this cabinet was more cohesive meant that it had a much narrower power base. The patrons were limited to President Wahid and Vice President Megawati and excluded Amien Rais and Akbar Tandjung, although PAN and Golkar did have people in the cabinet. The cabinet members from PDI-P, who were supposed to be Megawati's people, were also loyal to Gus Dur, so it became practically the cabinet of Gus Dur. There was no problem with that at first because Megawati was clearly a member of Gus Dur's team. But the supporters of Megawati, especially those who joined late in the hope of getting on her political bandwagon, were uncomfortable with this situation because it didn't get them anywhere in gaining a foothold on power. Since Gus Dur did not allow empire building within the government, Megawati's presence in the position of vice president didn't do much good for those who wanted to benefit from riding on Megawati's coattails.

People say that observations about her intelligence irritated Megawati more than outright political attacks. Soon there were leaks on comments Gus Dur might or might not have made about Megawati. This made it easier for people to lead Megawati into taking a position against Gus Dur, together with Amien Rais and people from the Akbar Tandjung camp.

By the beginning of 2001, these three camps solidified their opposition to Gus Dur and his party. At that time Gus Dur had two options: stick with his original agenda or compromise. And he choose the first one. He felt he had a strong cabinet and it would be successful as long as he gave it a chance to work. Also, he felt that further political compromise with the opposition would be futile as that strategy proved to be ineffective the first year.

Besides, we needed to get along with reform, the cleaning up of the military, the acceleration of the justice process for corruption and also getting the human rights violators into some sort of tribunal—preferably at the domestic level. The more insistent Gus Dur was on his political platform of reform, the more enthusiastic the opposition group became as they knew they would not be included in such a platform.

When Baharuddin Lopa came on board as attorney general in June 2001, the line of demarcation became very clear: reform on one side and status quo on the other. But when the press chose to be on the status quo side, the battle became next to impossible. Their biggest issue remained the decree which Gus Dur tentatively kept mentioning since January 2001 on possible scenarios if Parliament and the Assembly were to violate the constitution. These scenarios included suspending Parliament and calling for fresh elections. Although it was an elegant idea at a theoretical level, it did not meet with much support from political groups. The military and police were strongly opposed to it as well because they felt they would not be seen as being on the side of reform. I was one of the people who supported Gus Dur in maintaining his position on the decree, believing that the message of reform had to be carried through to the end.

෴

The Final Blows

I knew Gus Dur's government was doomed when I saw the lengths to which his political opponents were willing to violate laws and ethics to get him out of office. Every time Gus Dur made a statement of principle, his political rating with Parliament went down. As I knew Gus Dur would never give up his political principles, I felt that it would only be a matter of time until he was be forced out of office. But I could never tell when that would happen. Hope against hope, I half-expected a political miracle might happen. It's all right to hope for a miracle—you just shouldn't depend on them. Besides, the other alternative would be to compromise on principle, and that would mean forsaking the hope—however distant—that Indonesia could be home to a decent society.

The anti-Wahid cabal tried to get him for everything and ended up with nothing. The Bulogate accusation failed, just as Bruneigate failed. They tried to find weakness in the way the president appointed the new police chief Chaeruddin. At the end they just dropped the pretence. They replaced him with Megawati because they were fed up with him. Or maybe because Marsillam was appointed Attorney General, and they would be in jail in the next few weeks if they didn't hurry up and protect themselves. It sounds petty, but after observing Indonesia's current day politicians I would not rule out that kind of reasoning.

They made all the rules for Memorandum I & II and the special session—but in the end they just dropped everything and dismissed him. They started with flowers and soft music, and when it didn't work, they just ganged up and raped the presidency. And when the military would not play their constitutional role, they just turned around and disobeyed their commander-in-chief, which is technically a coup d'etat. Having had that decision established as a formal Assembly decision, we accept the political reality. But we have to live for tomorrow, and encourage clear perspectives even when we cannot have them supported by the majority.

Playing a game of classifying the ethical profiles of people in political cast of characters, it is quite satisfying that the bad guys are generally on the other side, the ones with the most corruption, the ones with the most human rights violation, the cynical politicians. On our side we had innocent and naïve people who still longed to have a better society. People like Baharuddin Lopa encapsulated the Gus Dur winds of fresh change, our Prague Spring, almost two years of very heady-clean air, fresh air followed by return to a stuffy and malodorous reality.

Questioning governmental performance in an acrimonious political environment is an arbitrary exercise. If you're playing tennis, you have to play according to accepted rules (unless you're like Bobby Riggs who played tennis as a wager while holding an umbrella, tied down to a chair and wearing a raincoat). It is difficult to measure a president by the measure of economic reform he has achieved when the ministers are not on the same team as the case was in the first cabinet, when other ministers turn out to be supporters and now members of the cabinet formed by his rivals.

It is not productive to return to the debate on government performance. We should look to the future and see what we can learn from our experience. While we accept political defeat, we should not discard the remaining dreams of reform. They have to be conveyed to the people and not to be destroyed—like Soeharto destroyed alternative points of view during his tenure. The Wahid presidency was destined to fail from the beginning, because Gus Dur would not play the political game. We just hope since he is out of power, the need to assassinate his character should be gone.

People are still providing analysis that everything went wrong because of Gus Dur. I say things went wrong *despite* Gus Dur. It is easy for people to second-guess after the fact. Many of the reforms Gus Dur brought have gone unnoticed. Who could have ousted Wiranto in such a delicate manner, making him defensive on human rights violations? No other politician could legitimize the presence of the ethnic Chinese, release religious ideas into the open, make an extraordinary effort to normalize relations with Israel, take a rational look at *all* intellectual thought (including Marxism), and generally push for freedom, tolerance and compassion on every front. These things did not happen on their own.

The presidential office did not run well. It could not have without the cooperation of the bureaucracy. Once inside the palace I could see compromise did not work but the reverse was useful, of making a sharp line of demarcation like Lopa did. When we tried to cooperate with parts of the old system like the Golkar party, we met with disaster. It was Golkar who, in the last days, misled the president to the insupportable appointment of the new police chief, Chaeruddin. The recommendation came straight from Golkar leaders Akbar Tandjung and Marzuki Darusman. It happened like this:

When Bimantoro put the police force in limbo by refusing to accept his well-deserved dismissal, President Wahid had to appoint a new chief of police. But, given the sensitive nature of the issue, the timing had to be just right. On that Friday afternoon he had decided to postpone the ceremony to appoint Chaeruddin because the timing was off. I was getting ready to announce the delay to the press, when Marzuki came in to the president's office and conveyed the word from Akbar that we could go ahead and appoint the new police chief, albeit on an interim basis.

I was sitting there next to Marzuki, both of us facing the president as he reversed his decision based on Akbar Tandjung's recommendation. President Wahid was in fact so skeptical that Marzuki connected him to Akbar on his mobile phone. I didn't hear Akbar's voice, but I heard Gus Dur say, "So you think it's okay or shall we stall the appointment?" Apparently Akbar gave the green light and the president asked Marzuki to draw up the letter of appointment. I said, "Well, for once Akbar shows statesman-like behavior."

When President Wahid mentioned in his official inauguration address of the new Acting Chief of Police that the decision concurred with the approval of Parliament Chairman Akbar Tandjung, I whispered to Marzuki, "Ouch, do you think Akbar will like being made jointly responsible?" Marzuki said, "Don't worry. If he doesn't, I will take care of it." Of course we know that Akbar did deny his approval of the appointment, and Gus Dur was left unprotected from the forthcoming attacks of Assembly Speaker Amien Rais. In fact it became the newest reason to impeach President Wahid.

Gus Dur trusted Marzuki more than he did Akbar. To me they are the same. I like Marzuki, he is cool and reasonable. But I know he is a professional politician whose work is not based on trust. Gus Dur always said that Marzuki was a good intermediary with Golkar. I never objected to these personality judgments of Gus Dur. In the end we have to rely on our own instincts. It is a game of survival, of maximizing your options. I have no hard feelings against these kinds of people, because everybody plays the same game. They are better and most successful than most, they always come out on top. But to me that kind of success does not mean much.

People ask why these parliament members were so eager to push Gus Dur out of office. Some were actually angling for cabinet seats in a Megawati government. Others needed to escape impending prosecution. In one person's case the change of president made the difference between facing a corruption trial and being a respectable Deputy Chairman of the Assembly. It was a choice between heaven or hell.

The end of the Wahid presidency was sudden yet expected. I remember when I was standing by my mother in December 1977. She had a cardiac condition and became terminally ill. Everybody knew in his or her rational mind that her days were numbered. But somehow you prayed for a miracle. You hoped the doctors were wrong and that she would survive. But she did not. When death came it was very sudden—like death always is—but on the other hand we also realized it was coming. The expected moment came in an unexpected way.

That is why I was out of the country when the president was pushed out of office. Gus Dur thought I should keep my schedule to deliver that lecture in Sydney. I thought I could be away for a few days as the special session was scheduled for 1 August, long after my 25 July commitment. But we also knew every time somebody declared against President Wahid that his political chances became slimmer, especially when the other side started to take on a heterogenic look. Everybody under the sun joined the conspiracy, a lynch mob to get rid of Gus Dur and divide the political spoils.

I guess the longevity of his presidency was first challenged when Amien Rais appeared at the palace and agitated the crowd with battle cries using religious extremism. This was in January 2000 and it put Gus Dur on the political hit list. Since then Amien Rais has spent every ounce of his political energy to remove President Wahid. Gradually other parliament leaders joined in the feeding frenzy. The issues changed but the goal was unmistakable: get the president, under any pretext. By that time Parliament and the Assembly were repeatedly violating rules, laws and even the constitution. But such was the power of the press and vested interests behind it that the end justified the means. The leaders of the nation's supreme legislative councils had become judge, jury and executioner.

The coiled tension went off following the appointment of the acting chief of police. Reporters swarmed around the Assembly chairman's office to get his comment on this latest initiative by the president. Chairman Amien Rais at first was nonchalant in his reply, but as he was preparing to reply to a Dutch journalist and others, he was called into quarters by PDI-P parliamentary leader Arifin Panigoro. After fifteen minutes Amien emerged and to the amazement of the journalists spoke in a startlingly different tone. President Wahid's appointment of the acting chief of police, said Amien, was inexcusable. The Assembly should convene on the next morning, Monday 23 July, to demand accountability from the president. At that point the president's fate was sealed.

Most were shocked when President Wahid finally issued the decree to suspend Parliament on that dramatic night of 22 July. I thought it was a shining moment in his presidency because Gus Dur showed what he stood for without regard to his political survival. He could have chosen the easy way out and run to political safety by capitulating on principle. Instead he gave his message loud and clear: democracy has to be protected as a matter of morality and not expedience. I think the best time of the Wahid presidency was the last few months when he made our mission clear. I had the honor of making the press statement to the effect that we had to reform without compromise, the one which Minister Susilo Bambang denied as being official policy. The point is that while Gus Dur tried in the beginning to please everybody on a path of gradual reform, when the crunch came he stood fast and held his ground against corruption, against violation of human rights.

Clearly Gus Dur's actions did not stand up politically, but for the first time in our history we had a president who stood up for what is right. When Gus Dur was ousted I knew the Indonesian people would soon realize that they missed out on something good. In Australia I received SMS messages, e-mail and telephone calls that described the flood of people that besieged the palace—thousands coming to express support and sympathy for a president so many appreciated and so many misunderstood. In a flash, all the wonderful moments of sincerity and commitment of Gus Dur and the good people around him flashed around in my mind's eye as I floated down an emotional chute. These are the feelings I had when I wrote Gus Dur an email from Sydney as I digested the tragedy in that fateful week in July. Sadness I had never felt before as the world caved in, banishing our dreams of the Wahid presidency and the new society it should have brought. More than anger, there was a sense of loss that we were about to lose the invigorating ideas and mental energy that brought humor and good cheer to Indonesian political life for a brief shining moment. There was also gratitude that we as a nation had been granted a vision of what we could be.

My hosts at the of New South Wales Centenary of Federation Committee were extremely kind to me as Anna Roache, our excellent host, adapted a hotel room to become a press center to help me cope with the dozens of requests for interviews on the fall of the Gus Dur presidency. Australian newspapers, radio and television recorded history in a far more comprehensive way than by any coverage I have seen since. But I choked when I tried to talk to President Wahid on the phone. So on another sleepless night I just sat down and wrote him a short message. As I sent off my e-mail from my notebook computer in the hotel room at 3 o'clock in the morning, tears were streaming down my cheeks. I learned later it was read to the president by his good friend Greg Barton. The text, in its English translation, read as follows:

To: Abdurrahman Wahid <presiden@ri.go.id>
From: Wimar Witoelar <wimar@perspektif.net>
Date: Tuesday, 24 July 2001 03:05
Subject: Gus Dur, Thank You

> Gus Dur has shown us what is possible. If we fail for now, it is because that we do not know how to match him smartly. Gus Dur has opened our doors to a world never before seen in Indonesia. We were reluctant to step through those doors.

Gus Dur is the breath of freedom, pluralism, humanism. For several moments Gus Dur gave us a government clear and firm in its stand against corruption and violence. We have experienced the 'Prague Spring,' a window of freshness between two orders of hypocrisy and greed.

Had we not seen a total collapse of political ethics last week, today we would be seeing corruptors facing the process of investigation and justice. Now they can breathe with relief. Violators of human rights may still build their political fortresses. Had we not been betrayed, today we would still have the luxury of a great man as president. He gave us self-confidence, moral cleansing, a human dimension we have never felt as a people.

Political failure reminds us that we must not be narrow in our support of a great man. At the end we learn that we must support a humanistic president, and not compete with our egos. We realize that we must not be neutral in facing the collective crime of a political order. The political conspiracy of those who destroy the nation cannot be challenged by intellectual coyness.

To me personally, Gus Dur has shown that there is truly a public person I can admire and respect, a leader I can love with all my heart. Gus Dur is my father, my brother, my teacher, and my closest friend in jest. Gus Dur has shown us that we may conduct affairs of state with gentleness, cheerfulness and spontaneity.

Thank you, Gus Dur.

PART THREE

NO REGRETS

Saturday Night out with the Wahids

How could you have regrets working with a man like Gus Dur? I remember one day in August 2001, just three weeks after Gus Dur was ousted from office. That afternoon Munib Huda, Gus Dur's loyal personal assistant, called to invite me to join Gus Dur and appear with him and Jaya Suprana, the pianist and humorist, at festivities to be held by a group called the Urban Poor.

We came in three cars. Gus Dur, Yenny and I were in one car, *Ibu* Nur and their youngest daughter, Inayah, were in the other car, and the third was filled with other relatives and staff. The cars were asked to park a distance away from the stage where the activities were going to be held. We were provided with three *becaks*, three-wheeled pedicabs. One for Gus Dur, one for *Ibu* Nur and one for myself. I do not really like to be put on the same level with the former president of Indonesia, but as I still had a sore back I thought it was wise to take the *becak* rather than walk in the dark, stumbling over uncertain terrain. The welcome was very warm. People were cheering and laughing and banging things around, taking Gus Dur by the hand. It was joyous to see that.

We climbed up the stage, except *Ibu* Nur who was carried upstairs. Gus Dur was carried upstairs in his *becak*, it was really festive. On stage, Ibu Nur and Gus Dur sat down in their respective vehicles. He in his *becak*, and *Ibu* Nur in her wheelchair. I stood behind them, because this time I decided I should stand up. Next to me was daughter Yenny, and slightly to the back was Ina, the youngest.

The program was warm and honest. Jaya Suprana showed his sensitivity to the occasion and showed both his musical artistry as a pianist as well as his compassion. He had arranged a very simple program where he would accompany Gus Dur in traditional songs and translations from Arabic songs. These songs teach you how to deal with diversity, how to face a difficult life, and how to be in control of yourself. Gus Dur alternated singing with casual exposition of his thoughts, advice and commentary; sometimes light, sometimes amusing and always very, very entertaining.

As he talked I watched the expressions on the faces of the people in the audience. Some of them were smiling, some of them were clapping their hands and many of them were in tears, either in joy or despair I don't know, but it was a very emotional meeting and we all felt very close.

After the event we stopped as a small, traditional restaurant, specializing in the Semarang soybean cake delicacy called *tahu pong*. It became a regular family outing. I guess, the owner of the place and the staff must have been fascinated to see such a famous man just walk in and order soybean cakes, fried chicken and *soto*, the traditional soup. I had vegetables myself to make sure my diet was on track and just tasted some of the *tahu pong*. Honestly. The talk was really family-like, with Jaya Suprana keeping us all entertained. But the beauty of the evening did not dawn on me until much later. I had been with Gus Dur and his family many times over the ten-month period of my spokesmanship, and that evening felt very much like evenings we spent together when they were Indonesia's first family. It was not a step down to be an ordinary family just as there were never any pretensions when they became a presidential family. Gus Dur, his wife and their daughters talked to the waiters in the same friendly way they had before, during and after the presidency. Politically the ouster of the president was a traumatic experience, but in personal terms Gus Dur and his family took everything in stride. Such balance and poise meant very much to me and made for the best working climate anyone could ask for.

Something Good Must Come Out Of It

Good feelings are not everything. It is great to have no regrets but we must make something out of our experiences. Gus Dur was replaced in July 2001 and nothing has happened months later in the way of improvement. All the energy has been spent in putting the new president in place. The positions are filled but not used except for private and party consolidation. Dissidence in the provinces has not improved, freedom fighters are simply killed or silenced. The economy is stagnant and slipping backward in the vital areas of bank restructuring and privatization of state enterprises. Megawati's economic cabinet hangs like a computer failing to boot into its initial operations. The 'dream team', as some columnists dubbed Coordinating Minister for the Economy Dr. Dorodjatun Kuntjoro-Jakti and his economic ministers, has turned into 'the dreaming team'. The story is not over—and as the Americans say, it ain't over till the fat lady sings, and no fat lady has been singing lately.

One can only be grateful for the many positives that Gus Dur has brought to Indonesian political life, and that is why I have no regrets that we tried to play straight for the people, even flying headlong into the concerted opposition of the corrupt and violent regime of the past.

In a dramatic way the people of Aceh have responded to the challenge to be pro-active in seeking their own destiny, to the dismay of the people who look at the picture in narrow nationalistic terms. The fact that they now come out and say that they want a referendum and that they want freedom reflect a new consciousness which has never been seen in Indonesia.

In a nutshell, we have been brought out of the tunnel, except we do not know where we surfaced. This was a very long, dark tunnel. We have always had a light at the end of it, and finally we broke loose into that light. We don't know where we are, but at least we are above ground and the tunnel, in the meantime, has collapsed. There is no turning back and we might not be where we want to be, but we can make our way much more easily.

Even if the government has slipped us back into the remains of the tunnel, they are government that we can cope with. We face a lot of challenges. We have to be pro-active about meeting those challenges, and if we are smart we won't have to look behind our backs. If violence and corruption still go on, it should not be in the name of the government. Having said that, we know that Megawati is vague in her direction, but we can define our own direction as a society. It is the beginning of a new age. Success depends on whether we can make use of our freedoms. Because if not, there will always be the old model that people try to revive. The model of absolute power and coercion has not disappeared. It is back at center stage, but we are no longer just the audience.

One month after Gus Dur became the president, the public responded to the new freedoms. The Human Rights Commission team on East Timor came up with results confirming stories which had long been circulating in unofficial form: the militia and the pro-Indonesia forces had and butchered villagers and burned down villages at the encouragement of the military. This was the stuff of informal stories in Indonesia only reported in parts of the international press. The Gus Dur government approved as an Indonesian commission declared its findings with witnesses that they claimed were credible, saying it was General Such and Such in the Indonesian army who had been taking the initiative in these atrocities. On top of that, the Commission planned to interrogate these generals— four or five very big names including Wiranto himself, for which they were asking for the president's permission. At this point President Wahid contributed to the solution by dismissing Wiranto from the cabinet after he had been placed there as a concession to the Golkar and military forces. It is ironic that five months after Megawati became president, her contribution was to initiate the release of Soeharto from prosecution. Such is the contrast between the two presidencies.

It was a long way from the human rights action to economic recovery, justice, legal reform, but the important first steps were taken in the right priority. Equally Gus Dur's initiatives in foreign relations were elegant, although speculative and aggressive. But they showed great imagination. Too bad the people could not match that with equal foresight and determination. Many could not understand the trips abroad and the controversies that accompanied Wahid's initiatives. But the fact is that they were always taken in a transparent manner in the light of public scrutiny. It was a rocky road, a tumultuous trip. At that time I said it was like whitewater rafting: not for the timid and your have to just hold on and try to enjoy the journey. I think that most of the foreign policy initiatives were justifiable. Prior to the Wahid presidency we had completely lost our souls as a people. Described as barbarians by the Germans, stereotyped by foreign media establishments, Indonesia was a pariah among nations, and then it became known as the world's third largest democracy.

A Word to the Media

It is an understatement to say that President Wahid was a victim of the media. It was a hot and cold relationship, and in fact much praise has been given to Gus Dur for his intellect and vision. Articles, books and film documentaries will assure Gus Dur of an honorable place in history. But in the day-to-day political press, most Indonesian and international publications joined the lynch mob against a president who represented too much uncertainty, especially those who had a stake in the status quo. People like Korean Prime Minister Kim Dae-Jung cautioned President Wahid against the media as they were often unsupportive or indifferent to the reform agenda of changemakers. Many publications in Indonesia had clear lines to protectors of the corrupt underbelly of Indonesia's public structure. Yet Gus Dur never even contemplated closing the lid on the press. In a few isolated instances he would talk about suing some newspapers for outright false information. But it would still be framed as a legal lawsuit without using the pressure of presidential power. Even then these lawsuits never came into being.

As a public person, Gus Dur has been close to the press throughout his adult life, but he received very bad treatment from the media throughout his presidency. The domestic media is in a state of flux and captivated by the euphoria of a free press. But surprisingly the international press also came through with a very strong bias in some cases. It happened to even the best of publications including the world-renowned *Newsweek* magazine. There had been good understanding with this personal favorite of mine until Lally Weymouth came along.

Reporters are trained to be sharp, humorous and skeptical. In short, witty. Unfortunately cynicism is the twin of wit, and it is amplified when reporters do not know their subject well. Add an excess of ego and some writers become downright disparaging. I was astounded by my experience with Elizabeth (Lally) Weymouth, who came to Jakarta to have a special interview with President Wahid. She is *Newsweek*'s senior reporter and happens to be the daughter of *Newsweek* owner, Katharine Graham. I enjoyed meeting Ms. Weymouth. But her writing on this occasion seriously taxed my lifelong respect for her mother's magazine.

Take the phrase that she wrote in the 28 May 2001 article 'A Turning Point For Indonesia'. Ms. Weymouth wrote, "Wahid's view was not shared by anyone I met on a recent trip to Indonesia." I don't know how many people she managed to talk to during her stay of a few days in Jakarta, but knowing her schedule it could not have been more than ten. What kind of people were they? I know at least four were people who had turned against the president for various reasons. I was also amazed at the tone of authority with which she reported on a delicate political process in Indonesia. The amazement was complete as Ms. Weymouth had admitted that it was her first-ever trip to this country. With her busy schedule interviewing world-famous personalities it is excusable that she had superficial knowledge of Indonesian issues and no experience with its culture. Her interviewees had to be able to speak English and be culturally amenable to meeting an American powerhouse of the press.

The culture gap showed as I was arranging Lally Weymouth's interview with the president. It repeated a routine I had gone through some months before, which ended in an anticlimax. Just as we had juggled the president's schedule around to accommodate Ms. Weymouth's schedule, she cancelled out in preference for a story in Africa. I breathed a sigh of relief until she reappeared. This time she really meant it, she insisted she had to interview the president. I had a mutually respectful relationship with *Newsweek* personnel around the world and received calls from Washington; Bangkok, Beijing and Jakarta to give Ms. Weymouth another chance. I realized the importance of the interview when they kept checking me—separately—to be assured that the interview was still on. Of course it was. My appointments do not disappear into thin air. "Well," one of them said at one point, "we heard it was cancelled." It took me some patience to explain

*Newsweek's Lally Weymouth, daughter of Katharine Graham,
kept her aggressive manner as Southeast Asia Bureau Chief Ron
Moreau looked on. My colleagues left the room as they could not
bear to see the president being treated so rudely.*

that whatever they heard somewhere, I was the one
responsible for press appointments and as far as I was
concerned, there was no change. I thought America was
the least feudal of societies but then to my incredulity the
presidential office got a call from the US Ambassador
asking us to provide time for Ms. Weymouth. That kind
of bureaucratic kibitzing was familiar in the Soeharto time
here, but it was hardly to be expected from the most
modern society in the world.

Ms. Weymouth showed up at the appointed time,
after reports came to me over my cellphone that she was
giving some palace staff a hard time for not being on the
ball. It confirmed my earlier discovery that Soeharto-style
feudalism is not the exclusive domain of old bureaucratic
bosses.

In many respects the interview itself went well
except that her New York accent and toughness threw
Gus Dur off-balance in the beginning, and mistakes of
hearing happened on both sides. A top official who sat in
on the meeting left midway because he could not accept
the president being, in his words, "barked at"—but did

not want to override my authority in allowing the
interview to continue. All these things made for an
ambience unfit to discuss a delicate subject. True enough,
the published interview made heavy play of Gus Dur's
mistakes in interpretation and was used by *Newsweek* to
bolster their impression of him as having gone the way of
Richard Nixon. "The Indonesian president seems willing
to cling to power at any price," she wrote about the
showdown between President Wahid and Parliament.
Very little attention was paid by her or *Newsweek* to the
flagrant disregard of ethics and the law that anti-Wahid
parliamentarians have constantly shown in their cabal
against him. To my knowledge the US Congress did not
have this weaknesses in their confrontation with President
Nixon in 1974-1975, nor did Richard Nixon have the
distinguished record of human rights and democracy
activism Gus Dur had built up over decades.

Clichés that build up the image of an irresponsible Gus
Dur showed up very often in the general press, although
seldom in in-depth articles about Indonesian society. It
might well have been a convenient format for the
continent-a-week roving journalist. Some members of the
press loved to prey on the statements of Gus Dur for their
own purposes, whether simply for amusement or for
targeted sensationalism. It was almost as if they were
working backwards from some popular notions about
President Wahid to generate interesting articles. We came
to know some very good foreign journalists who were
astute and informed on the true issues facing Indonesia's
democracy. But some foreign journalists, usually those who
are not based in Indonesia, took particular glee in depicting
a 'messy country' and a messy leader to imprint their image

of Indonesia as 'the worst place to be' in the minds of the unsuspecting public. Ironically the loudest protestations against these negative clichés often came from expatriates residing in Indonesia. Sure this is a place with plenty of troubles, they would say, but there are positives behind the negatives. It was clear that reality in the mind of the media is couched in terms of maximizing bylines and pushing conventional and convenient stereotypes. The daily lives of people in the country and development processes are too subtle for stories to be carried in the competitive media marketplace.

It was also popular for publicity seekers to come up with instant analysis of Gus Dur's psyche. Here in Jakarta, a psychiatrist came up with a psychiatric analysis without even having a one-on-one evaluation. That is nothing new, but the sad thing is that this piece of cheap attention-seeking was picked up by parliament members and members of the press. Seth Mydans, the respected, Bangkok-based senior journalist for the *New York Times*, described the way Gus Dur's mind works in a post-Wahid presidency article in the *Times*. It is strange that a journalist thinks he can define the thinking processes of another man. Mydans wrote that Gus Dur's mind seems to run on parallel tracks and that he jumps from one track to the other based upon his own imagination.

Mydans also wrote that Gus Dur has been often confusing to even his countrymen although now he is not listened to by as many people. One wouldn't say that about former President Clinton that now he is not listened to by as many people as before, because it is understood if the person is no longer president then not as many people listen to him. Actually, I am not convinced that less people are listening to Gus Dur. Since his removal he has been in ever higher demand as a public speaker and many of his pronouncements have proven to be true after his dethronement.

Freedom of the press is paramount in the world and also in Indonesia. I would be the first one to defend it, but it frightens me that a reporter could take a casual conversation with a man known to be mischievous with words and then write an article with such grave implications. The article even hinted at a possible military coup and implied approval by Gus Dur, the man who has stood up to the Indonesian military and worked with reformist elements inside to cleanse it of its bloodstained past.

The *New York Times* is a newspaper with one of the best reputations in the business. For me it has been a source of news and intellectual stimulation ever since I became aware of the world in the mid-sixties. Through the years of the Vietnam War and the cases dealing with civil liberties in the United States the *Times* has been for me the epitome of an enlightened press. So it was a great awakening to find out that the *Times*, along with other great newspapers like the *Washington Post* and respected publications like *Newsweek* which have great credibility and deserving good reputations, have become such powers unto themselves. I thought at that time I would talk to Seth Mydans who I know is a good person, but I found out it went beyond the individual reporter. The damage went beyond undoing when the *Wall Street Journal* came out with a strongly worded editorial telling Gus Dur to stop talking, referring to Seth Mydans' article.

The difference which is emerging between senior reporters like Mydans and some of the younger ones coming from countries like Australia is that the latter are willing to look at a new truth emerging. Context and culture are better understood by sensitive reporters who have the courage to question the labels stuck on Gus Dur and measure the real impact of the current leaders in Indonesia.

No doubt it is convenient for the reporter eager to get stories published to confirm and strengthen images of an Indonesia that is colorfully described by the words of Tom Friedman, the famous *New York Times* columnist, as a 'messy country'. Being a columnist with a specific flavor of his own, I can fully understand his desire to provide tongue-in-cheek wisdom on each country that he visits. For a hard news reporter, this artistic license should be curtailed.

To take the words of Gus Dur, now a plain citizen, at face value shows carelessness in following complex people in a complex environment. I have heard similar words being spoken by Gus Dur, but I would interpret them in a different way than Seth Mydans. Gus Dur likes to expound on possible scenarios, mixing facts and analysis, and add to that some elements of irony and humor. I would not use that material as hard news, and neither would people who know the country and the person.

At the other extreme, you have a number of people—academics and senior journalists—who are knowledgeable about Indonesia. Invariably they provide a different picture of Gus Dur than that of an erratic, incompetent president. Professor Clifford Geertz, eminent anthropologist wrote for the *New York Review of Books* in the 11 May 2000 article entitled 'Starting Over':

If close-up, been-through-the-mill experience, as well as patience, agility, humor, and a refined sense of timing, is what

Indonesia needs, Gus Dur, who is the closest thing to a machine politician the country has, could be the man. Compared at various times to Peter Falk's Columbo, the Javanese shadow-play buffoon Semar, Chaim Potok's lapsed rabbi Asher Lev, Ross Perot, Yoda, and (by his defense minister) a three-wheel Jakarta taxi, Wahid would seem well equipped to weave his way through the densest sort of lunatic traffic.

"In whatever direction Gus Dur looks with his one good eye there seems nothing to do but hang in there, try something, stay loose, hope for the best, and above all keep moving. Nothing if not mercurial, nimble and ingenious, and, blithely unaware, or unconcerned, that his position is impossible, he seems made for the moment, however long—it could be days or years—the moment lasts.

While Gus Dur's moment was very short as president of what some call the most difficult country to govern, some things were done in that brief period. The *Australian Financial Review* came out with the following editorial titled 'Indonesian freedoms are to be applauded' in its 6 April 2001 issue:

There was a time when Indonesia's approach to presidential accountability involved waiting for a rare candid comment from the otherwise impassive former president Soeharto. Officials were reluctant to discuss policies because they could never be entirely sure what the president thought. Amid the turmoil surrounding the Government of President Abdurrahman Wahid it is easy to lose track of how much things have changed. In fact, Parliament members spend so much time grilling ministers these days - for both accountability and political expediency - that there are 160 draft laws waiting to be passed.

The new openness has been on display in Australia

this week, where the presidential spokesman, Mr Wimar Witoelar, has been filling some of the space that would have been occupied by Mr Wahid if he had not cancelled his planned visit. But Mr Witoelar has not bothered with Canberra and has instead spent his time talking to civil society - business people, academics and the media.

Political spin-doctoring is a predictable routine in advanced democracies, but it is a welcome change for a spokesman for a country like Indonesia to be able to speak frankly about his country's problems with the authority of the president.

Mr Witoelar says that after 32 years of totalitarianism, expectations for stable government should not be set too high. But he also says Indonesians are still full of enthusiasm for their new democracy, even if it looks ineffective from the outside. With Parliament set up to impeach Mr Wahid later this year, it can only be hoped that the commitment to democratic process is maintained on all sides of the struggle.

Often the media was supportive in helping me articulate President Wahid's position. In this sense my efforts in Sydney and frequent visits to Australia were not in vain. Most of the television and newspapers around the time of the impeachment of President Wahid presented my views in undiluted form. Hamish McDonald, Foreign Editor of the *Sydney Morning Herald* supported the perspective of Gus Dur as the victim of corrupt and authoritarian elements entrenched in Jakarta's elite-level politics, who used spurious grounds for impeachment. The *Herald* noted that I came out strongly in defense of my boss and deeply critical of the forces boosting Megawati to the leadership. As well as people with normal political ambitions, the *Herald* quoted me, they included many linked to corruption during the thirty-two year rule of former strongman Soeharto, some of whom were in the pipeline for prosecution. Too much has been contaminated by vested interests. "We are seeing a government which has tried in vain for the last almost two years to do what the people wanted them to do, which is combat corruption and seek justice against human rights violations," I was correctly reported to have said.

We were the people who were supported by crowds which sought to escape from the Soeharto tyranny which brought us massive corruption and murders, as well as human rights violations in our provinces including East Timor. We were still in the attempt to get serious about human rights trials and we were just at the point of bringing several alleged corrupt officials to court when this happened very hastily—by people who were either involved in these violations in the past or who were quite close and supportive. So in other words this is the Soeharto regime proving that it's not that easy for the Indonesian people to discard this thirty-two-year-old stamp on our history.

I was cautious about implicating Megawati herself, though I expressed disappointment that this former ally of Gus Dur in the struggle for democracy had found new 'friends' among Soeharto-era elements. "Megawati has never personally delivered a single statement about this whole affair," I said, and I continue to maintain that view up until this very day. "She had delegated that to various spokespeople, official and unofficial. I think she owes the people an explanation of how her party has behaved."

While McDonald noted worries about a possible backlash from Gus Dur's supporters—Nahdlatul Ulama has thirty million members, most of whom are concentrated on the island of Java—I responded that Gus Dur had urged his followers all along not to use violence. "We are trying very hard to prevent that," he said. Instead, Gus Dur would urge his supporters to join in a campaign for Parliament to account for itself by speeding up fresh elections not due until 2004. "We want to be behind a moral political movement at the grassroots and civil society level, because at the institutional and parliamentary level, too much has been contaminated by vested interests," I said. "There just isn't enough money in the rest of Indonesia to compete with that which is being spent by the political machine that is currently taking over the country."

In the end, what matters is the mutual respect I managed to retain in good measure. I don't think personal goodwill ever disappeared between the president and the press. Certainly for me the media people have been wonderful. For example, after the fall of Gus Dur I received a simple fax from CNN's Indonesian correspondent Atika Shubert. She gave me credit for always trying my best to provide access to the process, making the Wahid presidency a very open one. She also said something nice about me as being a special kind of presidential spokesman. Bless her. She supports my belief in Anne Frank's saying that deep inside, people *are* really good at heart.

With Friends Like These
On a quiet morning of conversation in his Ciganjur home a few weeks after he was removed from the presidency, Gus Dur made a remark about intellectuals, a term used in a loose way in modern-day Indonesia. The problem with Indonesia's so-called intellectuals, said Gus Dur, is that the more fame they get, the more they believe too much in their own worth. It had become such that for many so-

called Indonesian intellectuals truth has become personal-
ized; truth is how an intellectual perceives something.
People who would dare to see things in a different light
are hardly accepted in the intellectual community.
Challenges to truth as perceived by the intellectuals are
most often rejected rather than absorbed. At the time Gus
Dur was speaking, press office staffers Adhie Massardi,
Yahya Staquf, Al Zastrow, Santo Dewatmoko and
Lukman were present. Gus Dur went on to say, "that is
why Wimar Witoelar was never an insider with these
intellectuals, because he does not see things in an absolute
way." I responded, "Well, I never see myself as an
intellectual, I just see myself as somebody trying to make
sense out of things by applying the common sense of the
ordinary man."

I never saw myself as a heavyweight intellectual like
Goenawan Mohammad or Nurcholish Madjid. Heavyweight, yes (120 kilograms at one time); intellectual
sometimes. These people who became household names
are giants, role models of the newly empowered Indonesian people. The intellectuals presented themselves as
the reference point of Indonesian morality. When Gus Dur
was removed from the presidency and was preparing to
leave the palace, a group of activists loosely labeled as
reformists, human rights and environmentalists—all
members of the civil society—issued a supportive
statement and Goenawan, the 'dean' of the intellectuals
said, "Gus Dur, welcome back to civil society!" That
sounded like a warm and friendly welcome and we took
it as such. Still there was an underlying judgmental tone
there. Does Goenawan feel he is authorized to welcome
people back to civil society? Furthermore, it gave the
impression that Gus Dur had entirely left civil society and

was then coming back. It implied that civil society should be out of the power structure.

Goenawan is a man to be admired, a big contributor to the quality of the Indonesian psyche. But at a time when we have to apply all our faculties to concrete reform, it is disconcerting to have kibitzers second guessing every attempt to do something. Towards the end of the Wahid presidency, the feeling of self-importance had sadly degraded much of the reporting of the weekly news magazine *Tempo*—probably the best such publication Indonesia has ever had largely due to the talent and energy of Goenawan and his colleagues. *Tempo* was the soul of the democratic core of the silent majority when Soeharto had free rein over the country. They were even closed down by Soeharto in 1994 because of their independent position. Yet when Gus Dur was in trouble, *Tempo*'s Chief Editor Bambang Harymurti enjoyed ridiculing and castigating the president. It was sad to see that. *Tempo* did not take the role it had done so well in the past, showing its position on what is right and what is wrong. Instead they were out to make a point about power and its essential evil. Bambang, a sharp intellectual who is one of my dearest friends, always says that the function of the press is to 'empower the oppressed and oppress the powerful'. While that might be a snappy slogan, it diminishes the function of the press to provide a service to society. The problem is if we are to reform, it takes power. To assume legitimate power, you have to join the power structure. But if intellectuals see being in power compromises your integrity, then such dogmatism makes the reform process extremely difficult. The only one way to do things would then be by revolution. Gradual change requires some part of the intellectual elite to get their hands dirty and work within the halls of power. Actually this is what people did in 1966 with poor results in the long run, but still it had to be attempted up to a certain point. Now this has become the dilemma that has plagued the Indonesian *reformasi*. The good guys want to be the fairest in the forest while the bad guys steal the show.

Growing Stronger in a Soft State

Gus Dur is not a man who dwells on regrets. As far as I am concerned, we are very fortunate to have been given a chance to express to the world that the Indonesian people are not the negative types that you see always being depicted in the international media.

Some pundits say Indonesia is not ready for a democracy. I would say the people currently occupying the political institutions might not be ready for democracy, but the people are. Indonesia is ready for democracy, she needs democracy. But the politicians who are occupying the seats in the political institutions put more importance on their self-interest than on the nation's interests.

On corruption, President Wahid maintained his clean record. He tried to get the Attorney General to get come to grips with the problem. He threatened the previous Attorney General Marzuki Darusman many times that he would lose his job if he didn't shape up. And by the time he shaped up it was too late. Gus Dur replaced him with a very tough attorney general, but he tragically passed away just as he was preparing to take action. Baharuddin Lopa and his successor Marsillam Simandjuntak had already put the names of several suspected of corruption into the prosecution pipeline. They are now in limbo, taking vacation as Vice Chairman of the Assembly and

The nation's top law enforcers Police Chief Bimantoro, Attorney General Marzuki Darusman, and Justice Minister Baharuddin Lopa listened to the president's firm line: get some action or changes will have to be made.

other high positions. Unfortunately the Megawati government has not picked up those cases yet.

In the last months of the Wahid presidency he took to anti-corruption in pretty strong terms. In the first year it was not possible because he had to serve as a coalition partner with Megawati, Akbar Tandjung and Amien Rais. But when he was on his own and when I was there with him, he just took the straight road. Which of course took us right down the ravine. But at least the intentions were made clear. In summary of President Wahid, I would say he is the man who opened the door to show the Indonesian people what we can be. But nobody dared to step through the door because of fear of the unknown. We have confirmed that public opinion, media, the press are supreme; that it is important to follow the public, that you cannot rely on truth alone. The current president of Indonesia must believe that she cannot hide any scandal from the people, that you have to take empowerment of the people seriously. That would in fact be the legacy of the Wahid government. That he empowered the people to a surprising degree. As for me personally, I was just, as President Wahid said once to a delegation from East Java, a "cog in a machine." But I got the privilege of serving a great man, of being in the front row at a very historical time, learning about my country and learning about myself.

The priorities of the nation in terms of attention to an issue have been turned around and dominated by tabloid headline gossip. In a recent radio discussion, I mentioned that I don't really blame the media for this. In my view, it is as if the elements of society—using the metaphor of a magnet and iron filings—have lost their alignment with the disappearance of the magnetic field. The positives and the negatives are all heading in different directions now. In Soeharto's time, they were all perfectly aligned in the direction that Soeharto prescribed. Those that would not conform were eliminated, neutralized or otherwise rendered ineffective. This, we now realize, is an undesirable condition. What we would prefer is for the filings to be aligned according to the magnetic field of democracy and justice, the magnetic field of a civil society, of a sense of ethics between right and wrong. Instead, we had nothing. The only institution that truly functioned during the thirty-some years, ending in 1998, was Soeharto. When Soeharto was gone, there were no institutions. The government didn't work, the supreme court was stagnant, the legislature was defunct. Now they tried—or more correctly *we* tried—to fix this thing with the period of reform, but this was the first social experiment of that scale in a country of this size. It is understandable that the results had been far from perfect.

The governments have replaced each other in rapid pace, Habibie to Wahid to Megawati, and they're still not functioning entities (except for making officials more comfortable in their little fiefdoms). The Supreme Court was recently overhauled by Gus Dur, but even this didn't reach the core of this institution. The corruptors are still suspects, and certainly the recent decisions handed down by the new Supreme Court are far from inspiring.

As for the supreme legislative bodies, the Assembly and the Parliament, that is a totally different story. The Parliament and the Assembly that we now have in Indonesia, are bodies with the power of the people but without the heart of the people. When asked if indeed democracy is inappropriate for a country like Indonesia, I would not say anything to confirm that dangerous notion. Instead, I would say the institutions are a necessity. Democracy is not a choice but a must—it is imperative for *any* nation, especially for a nation trying to grow in its identity like Indonesia. In order for the institutions to function, however, they have to be occupied by people with proper ethical equipment. Unfortunately, that is not the current situation we have in Parliament and the Assembly. This leaves the public totally challenged, confused, and in some cases discouraged. People who had hopes for improvement when we departed a totally tyrannical system instead see more difficult times under a democratic system—a system which was abused by the very leaders the people chose.

To my mind, the problem is not with our nation, but rather with the state and its institutions that translate popular demand into managerial institutions. There is the dilemma: the Parliament does not speak for the people, the government does not act for the people, and the Supreme Court does not judge for the people. But the people do know what they want and the elements of a strong social system have been greatly improved. People like Karlina Leksono, or Esther Purba, or Teten Masduki—who were not known five years ago—are now in the forefront of public consciousness. They are leaders of thoughts, carriers of hope and actively doing things for the nation. At the moment they do not have an impact on the course of the nation, but that is because of the ineffectiveness of the institutions which I have just described.

In the same radio discussion, the host supported a simple concept I had been carrying around: the Concept of Ordinary People. The ordinary people ultimately will determine the social fabric of a nation. And we have many ordinary people. People who did not go along with the wave of corruption, collusion and violence in the Soeharto days. But ordinary people normally don't become heroes, i.e. the type who can sacrifice themselves for the public good. Although good and pure at heart, they are not freedom fighters.

These ordinary people are on the sidelines at the moment, because the playing field is jammed with the good guys and the bad guys. The good guys are the ones fighting against human rights abuse, the bad guys the ones corrupting society. The heroes versus the villains. The ordinary people are neither—just seeking a better life. They want to be rich, but they do not want to corrupt; they want democracy, but they could not die for it.

In the end, the ordinary people must prevail because even without realizing it, they are shifting the social norms of the country. The ordinary people are upset that Soeharto still commands such respect that his convict son is allowed to leave detention without 'cuffs. I can see the vast difference of public opinion n Tommy in 1996 and in Tommy in 2001. In 1996, he was riding around in a Rolls-Royce, wearing custom-tailored suits, followed by a string of admirers and isolating himself from the ordinary's people misery. It was difficult to conceive that such a prince as Tommy Soeharto could be a police captive and the subject of public contempt. Now *that* is a public sanction—a social sanction against a person and a family, to whom legal sanction is incapable of being applied.

Giving Direction to Megawati's Journey

As this book goes to press in early 2002, I feel the effort to democratize the country has lost steam and direction. They say that reform is a journey and a destination, and that the journey is more important than the destination. But now it has become a journey without a destination. People had hoped for a lot from the team of Gus Dur and Megawati. When that team broke up the hopes were dashed. In the change of the presidency, much of the negative aspects of our society came out, and the untested political system broke down. A lot of decisions were made which the nation is starting to regret. So we have a new government without a new spirit. Maybe more importantly than that, the regime that we tried very hard to put behind us, the Soeharto regime, is still ever-present in a new guise. We have very strong remnants of the Soeharto regime plus an embryonic political system which has broken down. Politicians are bickering among each other and forgetting that the real threats to the nation are violence, corruption and human rights abuse which are still being committed by the people who used to be around Soeharto.

From the beginning, President Wahid was doomed because he was made president by an unholy alliance whose only purpose in electing him was to block Megawati from becoming president. And that alliance had hoped that Gus Dur would play according to their tune. But when he asserted his independence and basic values of humanism and democracy, he lost the political support. The people who were threatened by the efforts in the last months of the regime to bring them to trial had no recourse to save their skins other than to get him out of power. So they lined up with a very big pool of people who did not understand what he was doing, who were confused by his ideas which were quite advanced for our political age. It was a string of communication problems plus concerted action from the old regime, plus ambitions of politicians who saw an easy way to power. All the bad elements of a political system came out and Gus Dur had to yield his position.

The Parliament and Assembly, the main responsible parties for the political drift of purpose, are like babies on a miracle drug. At the age of two they already act like they are forty. When they are still innocent in their values and unformed in their integrity they gained immense political physical power. And so they became an institution without morality. The morality stayed outside the political system. The Parliament and Assembly were disembodied from the will of the people who had elected them in 1999. In other words, they ran out of control. For good or bad, they took decisions quite distanced from what the public wanted. Witness that no huge support from the public came up, nobody rejoiced when Megawati replaced Gus Dur. Because it was just a political game on a very cynical stage.

As for President Megawati, she is the progeny of an illegitimate political process. Children of illegitimate unions must be given a chance, they should not necessarily be doomed. She does have a chance to repair the damage if she does well in her job as president, if she salves the wounds and finds a national consensus. The hope is that somehow people around her can make her realize that there's no way for the country to save itself than to find some unity based on proper values. Nobody gives trouble to Megawati if she goes three months without saying anything. Everybody gave trouble to Gus Dur every day when his every quote was searched for inconsistencies. The more he spoke the more confusing it became to people who are not used to seeing the truth behind the words.

People used to criticize the economics of the Wahid government. Compared to his performance in the first half of 2001, the results of the Megawati government in the second half of 2001 are quite dismal. Hers is a do-nothing government, privatization without action, hoping for things to fall into place based on the charm of her smile. At least during Gus Dur's time there was communication, and I don't think the IMF was necessarily that upset at the government because the agreement they are signing now is based on negotiations with his government. It's really not that bad in economics, and in politics people should give credit where credit is due.

Megawati, surprisingly, is not happy with Parliament although they gave up their scruples to put her in power. President Wahid was constantly attacked by Parliament, but it was not a problem because he never thought that the attacks were heartfelt or based on facts. We knew that they were based on misunderstanding and impatience and we have been proven right. Two months after he was pushed out of office, all the press have come to us and claimed to be good friends. So we never took it personally. We knew the press, the reporters; the editors could not by themselves face up to the pressure from the shareholders, the demands of the public for sensational press. Gus Dur never felt it was against him personally. As for his remoteness from Parliament, I would submit that it is Parliament which is remote from the people. If you took a poll in Indonesia now and tried to find out how many people think Parliament represent their interest, you would find your pickings to be very slim indeed.

While the Wahid presidency constantly suffered persecution by the press, Megawati is more fortunate. Her silent style—while it exasperates many—does not invite the virulent attacks which Gus Dur seemed to draw constantly. Still in substance the press is often critical at the government of President Megawati Soekarnoputri. The most significant issue is Megawati's reconciliation with leading figures of the Soeharto regime to the point ignoring their human rights record. In a year-end speech to the military she even told them not to worry about human rights abuse, just be firm. Some advocacy groups such as the vocal Petisi 50 and the National Commission for Missing Persons and Victims of the Violence (Kontras) accused the Megawati administration of making deals with influential members of the New Order regime in a bid to maintain power. Many see that there will be systematic efforts to revive the culture of the autocratic New Order regime. Kontras coordinator Ori Rahman criticized the five-month-old Megawati administration for sacrificing human rights in the effort to maintain security. The bloody incidents in Tanjung Priok in 1984 and the 1999 post-ballot violence in East Timor are two examples. Some Indonesian generals have been named as suspects in these cases, but to date they have never been sent to trial.

Another thing I don't understand is why President Megawati is trying to lift the charges against Soeharto.

That is the big question as this book goes to press. Maybe there is a lot of truth to the cliché 'silence is golden', perhaps even for the president of a large nation. When Tommy Soeharto was finally captured after more than a year as a fugitive from the law, the Jakarta police diverted attention from Tommy's prosecution to illogical rumors that Gus Dur had made some sort of deal with Tommy. These rumors were subsequently quashed, but the damage had been done in typical media lynch rule. On the contrary, on the issue of Megawati clearly making the ultimate concession to the Soeharto family, not many in the press signal wrongdoing on her part. Most blame her unpopular decision on her judgment, not on her morals. The silent get away with more than those who are openly expressive. I don't know if there is any correlation with perceived intelligence. Gus Dur was recognized to be a smart man and that is why they suspected him of plotting and scheming. Megawati is not accused of political manoeuvres which may well be an insult to her intelligence.

I hope we will not continue to be sidetracked from the job we started to do in 1998. We should refocus on the main issues of the economy and human rights. Our economy is in the doldrums because nobody is doing anything. The cases of human rights abuse, which have been dealt with in the Wahid government are now on standby. The bad guys are getting back into place, the bad money is becoming bigger and bigger. Our crisis is just beginning. If Megawati allows the country to slip back into the old culture then she risks losing all the good will she accumulated during the long years of political struggle against Soeharto. Her current disposition of being closed and non-communicative will only further alienate people. There appears to be no sincerity in her administration.

Soeharto's regime was also insincere but in some ways effective. So far Megawati's administration is insincere and ineffective—the worst of both worlds.

The Final Word

Some people say that Gus Dur changed upon becoming president, or that indeed there were two Gus Durs. I don't think that is true. Gus Dur tried to play a unique role in Indonesia's transition by projecting his human and social values into the presidency, but his impact was curtailed by constant politicking. While president, Gus Dur was not fully supported by the military and not strengthened by the political infrastructure. His presidency was engineered for him by the Central Axis who kept to themselves the right to support or remove the president. Tragically he suffered politically without being granted the benefit of the doubt by the very people who should support him, the civil society who are actually his natural constituency. They instead remained ineffective second-guessers who expected him to behave like a perfect president, ignoring the fact that nobody can be perfect and reformist at the same time. There were not enough people who could tell the difference between Gus Dur's intentions and results, too many who kept complaining. Ironically Gus Dur himself never complained about the hand he was dealt. In the ten months of our proximity I never heard him once complain about his blindness, and his wife never complained about her infirmities. They make do with what they have, trying not to worry others by making light of their problems. He is known as a light-hearted man. But I learned he was dead serious once I joined him as his spokesman. He knew he had to take the long shots in our desperate attempts to reform society. Unfortunately

East Timor leader Xanana came with his wife and baby. President Wahid often chuckled at the similarity between his nickname Gus Dur and Xanana's last name Gusmao.

nobody could operate at his level of risk taking, and many of his bold political gambits met with no response.

The civil society, the political parties and even the pro-democratic movement did not express their support in a useful way. NU gave support, albeit without comprehensive political action—the kind one needs to support a president.

Some say Gus Dur played political games. Perhaps, but I always looked at them relative to games others play. I thought the games that other people played were done without much good will, sometimes in a very cynical way to defend of the old system. Gus Dur's games, more often than not, were born out of necessity. He had to rely on his wits to get from A to B without a good vehicle, avoiding potholes and hostile ambush. Driving straight would get him nowhere. I never saw any evil intent during the time

I was with President Wahid. It is very easy to find fault in the Wahid presidency, especially if you forget who else was in the government contributing to the failure. Many cabinet members who were nominated by rival parties didn't exactly bend over backwards to strengthen the presidency of the nation. Those were the internal failure factors. Externally the Parliament, the political pressure groups and the press all had a hand in arranging the destruction of the Wahid presidency.

Gus Dur is a very talented, brilliant man, who was not given the privilege of being helped by professional middle-class managers. He is a man who seeks the truth often, if needs be, all by himself. He will always be there, doing what he always does: traveling around Indonesia and around the world, making speeches two hundred days a year, receiving people who seek advice, trading jokes, living the life of a renaissance man. He is blessed with a very rich and fulfilling life and he is a much happier man than the politicians who snuck up on the nation and stole its spirit.

Gus Dur's major achievement was to show us that it *is* possible for Indonesia to rise above the image of a barbaric society. All by ourselves, we elected a president who supports human rights, who is a pluralist, an intellectual, a leader who opened the door to a better world for the entire nation. He showed us something that is precious about Indonesians—that fundamentally we are all good at heart. He showed the us that East Timorese leaders, Acehnese activists and former political prisoners can find some faith in the government, or at least in the president. *That* is Gus Dur's legacy: he showed us what is possible.